"God's greatest gifts to us are alw[...]  this book will help you unwrap your [...] but even more, you will be deeply en[...] ater for the thirsty soul, and that is [...] 'am Vredevelt, a woman of unique wis[...]

DR.
SENIOR PASTOR, EAST HILL CHURCH

"This is a sensitive, well-balanced book designed to encourage, inspire, and uplift the reader. It's sure to impact your attitude and outlook on the situations you're living with in a positive way. You will want to read the insightful chapters again and again."

H. NORMAN WRIGHT
BEST SELLING AUTHOR

"These inspirational stories will convince you that God is near in the darkest of times, eager to answer the cry of your heart with a miracle or with a flood of grace to sustain you in circumstances you don't understand. If you're feeling a bit overwhelmed, grab my friend Pam's book and pull up a chair by the fire—you won't be able to read it without having your heart warmed and your faith strengthened."

RON MEHL
PASTOR AND AUTHOR OF THE CURE FOR A TROUBLED HEART

"There are times life takes you down paths you do not want to travel and puts burdens on your shoulders you do not want to bear. Pam Vredevelt tells of her journey through such dark times with authenticity. She acknowledges her strong, turbulent, negative emotions and at the same time, the Lord's presence in the midst, meeting the deep heart needs. For those of you who know something of the 'valley of the shadow,' you will connect with this book and its message of life out of death."

PAMELA REEVE
AUTHOR OF FAITH IS...

"Pam knows that life is as hard as the ground we walk on. But she brings us to a place where we can take our shoes off and jump into cool, refreshing water. It doesn't change the hardness of the ground, but it sure helps our journey. Not only does Pam write well, but she has a knack for letting us 'peek' into her life and others' for the sole purpose of displaying God's great love. The 'surrender' story in Pam's life helps us to surrender as well."

ANNIE HERRING
SINGER AND SONGWRITER, FORMERLY WITH SECOND CHAPTER OF ACTS

Other books by Pam Vredevelt

Empty Arms: Emotional Support for Those Who Have Suffered Miscarriage, Stillbirth, or Tubal Pregnancy

Mothers and Sons: Raising Boys to Be Men (with Jean Lush)

Women and Stress (with Jean Lush)

Surviving the Secret: Healing the Hurts of Sexual Abuse (with Dr. Kathy Rodriguez)

The Thin Disguise: Understanding and Overcoming Anorexia and Bulimia (with Dr. Frank Minirth, Dr. Debra Newman, and Harry Beverly)

To schedule Pam Vredevelt for conference speaking you may write:

Pam Vredevelt (Conferences)

P.O. Box 1093

Gresham, Oregon 97030

MVFOL

ANGEL BEHIND THE ROCKING CHAIR

Stories of Hope in Unexpected Places

PAM VREDEVELT

Multnomah Books *Sisters, Oregon*

ANGEL BEHIND THE ROCKING CHAIR
published by Multnomah Publishers, Inc.

© 1997 by Pam Vredevelt

International Standard Book Number: 1-57673-644-X

Cover illustration by Sergio Martinez

Printed in the United States of America

Most Scripture quotations are from:
The Holy Bible, New International Version (NIV) © 1973, 1984 by International Bible Society,
used by permission of Zondervan Publishing House

Also quoted:
New American Standard Bible (NASB) © 1960, 1977 by The Lockman Foundation
Scripture quotations marked (NKJV) are taken from the New King James Version
© 1979, 1980, 1982 by Thomas Nelson, Inc. Used by permission. All rights reserved.
The King James Version (KJV)
The Living Bible (TLB) © 1971 by Tyndale House Publishers, Inc.
Scripture quotations marked (NLT) are taken from the *Holy Bible,* New Living Translation,
© 1996. Used by permission of Tyndale House Publishers, Inc., Wheaton, Illinois 60189.
All rights reserved.
The Holy Bible, New Century Version (NCV) © 1987, 1988, 1991 by Word Publishing,
Dallas, Texas 75234. Used by permission.
The Message © 1993 by Eugene H. Peterson
The New Testament in Modern English, Revised Edition (Phillips) © 1972 by J. B. Phillips
Scripture quotations marked (AMP) are taken from *The Amplified Bible Old Testament*
© 1965, 1987 by The Zondervan Corporation.
The Amplified New Testament © 1954, 1958, 1987 by The Lockman Foundation.
Used by permission.
Scripture quotations marked (MLB) are taken from *The Modern Language Bible*
© 1945, 1959, 1969 by The Zondervan Corporation. Used by permission.

ALL RIGHTS RESERVED
No part of this publication may be reproduced, stored in a retrieval system, or transmitted, in
any form or by any means—electronic, mechanical, photocopying, recording, or
otherwise—without prior written permission.

For information:
MULTNOMAH PUBLISHERS, INC.•POST OFFICE BOX 1720•SISTERS, OREGON 97759

Library of Congress Cataloging-in-Publication Data
Vredevelt, Pam W., 1955– Angel behind the rocking chair/Pam Vredevelt. p.cm. Includes
bibliographical references. ISBN 1-57673-644-X (paper) 1. Consolation. 2. Christian life.
3. Family—Religious life. 4. Vredevelt, Pam W., 1955– —Family. 5. Down syndrome—
Religious aspects—Christianity. I. Title.
BV4905.2.V68 1998 97-30277 248.8'6—dc21 CIP

99 00 01 02 03 04 05 — 10 9 8 7 6 5 4 3

*To those who have lovingly supported us as we have walked
a new path.*

*To the compassionate people in this world,
like the ones at the P.R.I.D.E. school, who are committed to helping
those with special needs reach their full potential.*

*To Easthill Church, for embracing our family, shaping our lives, and
reflecting the goodness of God.*

ACKNOWLEDGMENTS

John and I would like to thank our parents, grandparents, and extended family for the ways they have supported and encouraged us since Nathan's arrival. Their love and prayers have given us strength for the journey.

To the P.R.I.D.E. school staff for teaching us how to assist Nathan in his early years of development. You have shined the light on our path during dark days and given us hope for the years ahead.

Our sincere thanks to Pastor Ted and Diane Roberts, who have encouraged us in so many ways, but especially as they have coached us in the refinement and release of ministry. And to Pastor Ron Mehl, who, from across town, has touched our lives with his *agape* love.

There are some special youngsters who deserve a standing ovation for their availability to be Nathan's personal pal in the church nursery. To Lindsey Marsh, Janise Jensen, Sarah Berquist, Jessie Vredevelt, Tony Contreras, Katrina Ekwall, and Anna Ferrar—Bravo! for a job well done. And to Roxie, Reggie, and Becky our gratitude for making Nathan's introduction to regular preschool a smashing success.

John and I will be forever grateful to those who have lightened our load and made "time-outs" possible for us when our stress score was off the charts. Hugs and thanks go to the following people for loving our children while we refueled our tanks: Margaret and Leroy Nikander, Kelli Douglas, Celeste Miller, Bethany Smith, Jane Freeze, Eileen Kennedy, Doug and Marilyn Hume, and Sugar Carpenter.

To Larry Libby, my editor, who gave me the confidence to start writing again. The book was completed because he believed it was a redemptive message worth sharing. When I turned the manuscript over to him, I said, "I feel like a student handing my canvas, paints, and brush to the master artist." His creativity and word skills I believe are unparalleled. I consider him a mentor and feel privileged to have had the opportunity to co-labor with him.

Contents

CHAPTER ONE

AT THE YARN STORE

But He knows the way that I take;
when He has tested me,
I shall come forth as gold.
JOB 23:10, NKJV

It was just your typical trip to the yarn store.

Nothing monumental about the day. Nothing special about the mission. Kathy needed a few odds and ends to finish up a project or two. With her goal nearly accomplished, she found herself standing in front of some expensive white yarn, soft as a summer cloud—the kind she loved to knit into baby blankets.

She shook herself from the reverie. What was she doing? Baby blankets? She didn't need any more yarn. She turned to walk toward the cash register.

Something drew her back like a magnet.

Before she knew it, she was standing in front of the luxurious white yarn again. But why? It was so fancy. So impracticably expensive. *And so soft…so beautiful…so comforting for a new baby…*What baby? This was ridiculous. She didn't even know anyone expecting.

At that moment someone spoke behind her. "There is a special baby on the way. Make a blanket!"

Startled, she turned to see who it was. No one was there. The nearest person in the store was ten feet away behind the cash register, assisting a customer.

A special baby? What special baby? Then a thought hit her—like a surge of ice water through her veins. Kathy was the mother of three teenage girls. *Oh Lord, it isn't one of my girls, is it? Please don't let it be one of my daughters!*

Responding to the strange prompting, she bought the yarn and placed it on a closet shelf.

The following week she and her friend Marylee were sitting in church together. As the service began, Marylee leaned over and whispered, "John and Pam are pregnant again."

Kathy sat up very straight. Instantly, she understood.

"*That's* the special baby!" she blurted out loud, embarrassing herself. Then she whispered to her startled friend, "That's the special baby I'm supposed to make a white blanket for."

Following the service, Kathy caught me walking out the door and told me of her unusual experience in front of the yarn display. I didn't think much about that incident until the Lord pieced some things together for me in the hospital. Three days after Nathan was born, Dr. Eki, our pediatrician, returned from vacation and took charge of Nathan's care. I'll always remember his kind words after reviewing the case.

"Nathan is a very *special* baby," he told us, "and he has been given to very *special* parents."

I don't think his choice of words was a coincidence. I believe they were Spirit-inspired to bring clarity—and comfort—into our confusion and pain. I immediately remembered Kathy's trip to the yarn store, when God told her that a "special" baby was on the way. In the grief following delivery I found some relief, knowing that God was mindful of this little one while he was still in the womb—before our trauma even began.

John's story comforted me, too.

When I was five months pregnant, John was driving his

truck to our athletic club for his lunchtime workout. John loves to sing. And on this particular day he was listening to a praise tape, singing along at the top of his lungs.

The sun had chased away the Portland clouds. John felt good. He looked forward to some healthy huff and puff and sweat.

That's when it happened. In one world-stopping second, the vivid picture of a little boy with Down syndrome flashed across the screen of his mind.

"Oh God," he breathed. "Not that. I couldn't handle that."

And just that quickly the reply came back, *You can handle anything I give you.*

John hid that encounter in his heart for the next four months, uncertain if it was God speaking, or his own worst fears. But after Nathan was born, John knew it had been God who interrupted his worship in the truck that day. Today he believes God was trying to get his attention, to prepare him and give him confidence about what was to come.

You can handle anything I give you.

First Corinthians 2:9–10 tells us:

"No eye has seen, no ear has heard, no mind has conceived what God has prepared for those who love him," but God has revealed it to us by his Spirit.

Life is full of challenges, hardship, and suffering. These are the arenas in which we desperately need to hear from God. We need to know what the Spirit is saying. We need to listen.

Now that John and I are on the other side of grief, it's easier to see more clearly. Much of the emotional fog has lifted. As the days turn into months and years, John's encounter with God in the truck—and Nathan's soft white baby blanket—remind us to be sensitive to the Spirit's prompting. We're trying harder to give priority to what God says to us, over what we say to God.

Human reasoning, after all, won't reveal God's perspective. But if we're open to listen...His Spirit will.

CHAPTER TWO

GLORY IN THE BROKEN PLACES

*This priceless treasure we hold, so to speak,
in common earthenware—to show that the
splendid power of it belongs to God
and not to us.*

2 CORINTHIANS 4:7, PHILLIPS

Zena came into each session impeccably dressed in the latest
vogue, makeup designed to perfection. But the eyes that stared
at me were cold and hard as chiseled marble.

She had struggled with an eating disorder for nearly twenty
years, and she was one of the most bitter and controlling people
I ever worked with.

As we talked, I expected to uncover the source of Zena's bitterness. But the account of her childhood seemed rather typical
and uneventful. No great traumas. No major heartbreaks. Her
parents had a good marriage, and she spoke of a close relationship with both them and her two brothers. She butted heads
with the boys now and then, as most kids do in the healthiest
of families, but there was nothing out of the ordinary. Besides
being blessed with parents who loved each other, she also had
grandparents who lived next door, for added support. Her
grandmother was like a second mom and confidante, especially
during her teen years.

As I reviewed her history in that first session, I was puzzled.
The family dynamics didn't fit the common profiles of other
eating disorder patients. Wasn't even close. No divorce, no

abuse, no drugs and alcohol.... Neither parent was intensely rigid, perfectionistic, or driven. They were churchgoing folk who took life in stride.

A piece of the puzzle was missing. It had to be.

Details were colorful and vivid as Zena replayed her high school and college years. Cheerleading. Dance. Church choir. Gymnastics. 4.0 GPA. Scholarships. Sports awards. Titles.

Then, in her third year of college, everything changed. Trauma interrupted her life, and it became the hinge on which the rest of her life turned. That's when her reflections blurred, and the story became fragmented. That's the year her grandmother died...and the year when she was raped.

The loss of her innocence and the loss of her confidante were more than Zena could bear. The eating disorder became her tool to numb the pain, like an anesthetic. Gymnastics and college became a thing of the past. The bubbly brunette withdrew from life and went into hiding. For *years.* Eighteen years later she heard me speak at a conference about growing in hard places, and made an appointment the following week.

Zena spent several months in therapy, revisiting and processing the trauma she had tucked away as her secret. Facing and embracing her pain gradually diffused its power. Each week I saw change. Her cold stares were interrupted with tears and eventually...spontaneous smiles. Bit by bit, stone by stone, she dismantled the wall she had built around her heart and risked letting the pain out and letting me in.

In time, Zena gained the courage to join a therapy group I facilitated for women in recovery. One night the group wanted to talk about "God issues" and how they perceived God's involvement in their lives. I passed out paper and markers and asked the group to create a picture that illustrated their relationship with God.

One woman drew a stick figure of herself: no face, no hair or clothes, kneeling on one side of a stone wall that towered high above her. Her face was buried in her hands on the ground. Bright sunlight shone on the other side of the wall, where Jesus stood with scores of other stick figures. She described herself as someone who felt she was on the outside looking in.

"It feels like God has all kinds of friends down here on earth," she said, "but I'm not one of them."

As we went around the circle, each woman shared her picture. When it was Zena's turn, she held up a likeness of two very large hands, holding the handles of an ornate vase. The outline of the vase was carefully drawn and perfectly symmetrical. There were many colored markers she could have used, but she chose to do her picture strictly in black.

Down the middle of the vase she'd drawn a thick, jagged line, depicting a very deep crack. Her description moved me.

"This vase," she said slowly, "can't be fixed. The hands holding it are about to throw it away."

It wasn't a pretty picture, but even so, Zena had taken a step forward that night. For the first time in eighteen years, she was honest with herself and others about how she felt in her relationship with God.

I always marvel at God's sovereignty in putting groups together. One of the other members, Terry, immediately stepped in and asked Zena how the vase became cracked. Terry, herself a rape victim, "just happened" to be nearing the end of her recovery. Within the safety of the group Zena was able to uncover the shame-filled events she had hidden for years. I had a front row seat watching God do a deep work in Zena as group members offered her acceptance, grace, and truth.

Zena's bitterness began to change in subtle ways. It didn't happen fast, but then, long-term change rarely does. As the months passed, the eating disorder simply became less and less of an issue. Why? Because the pain driving the compulsion was losing its power. Zena had learned to face her pain and let it go, so there was less need for an "anesthetic."

One day Zena walked into my office. "I've made a decision," she said. "I want to be trained to work on the Rape Crisis Hotline." She didn't want others to suffer in silence as she had for so many years. She wanted to be a refuge for those who were scared and hiding. She wanted God to use her brokenness to help others heal. She wanted others to know there was hope.

Toward the end of Zena's recovery, the "God issues" came up again in group. I had saved the pictures from the time before and brought them out for review. Each of the women again received a clean sheet of paper and colored markers, and when they finished, they shared their new drawings with one another.

Zena's new picture intrigued me. Guessing at its implications, I felt a surge of excitement.

Once again she had drawn her perfectly symmetrical vase with swirly handles on the sides. Once again it was firmly gripped by the same two large hands. The deep crack down the middle of the vase was still there, too.

But she'd added something new to the picture.

Using the fluorescent yellow marker Zena drew heavy lines, like beams of light, spilling out of the flaw and flowing to the edge of the paper. Pointing to the crack, she said, "That's where God shines through."

As the others reflected on her drawing, one woman said, "Hey, it looks more like a trophy than a vase to me."

"Yes!" said another who knew her story. "You're in God's

hands. You're a trophy of His grace." The rest of the group nodded in unison.

Once again I was reminded that it is through our suffering, our trials, and our wounds that God's glory is often revealed. The subheading under Zena's vase could have said, "2 Corinthians 4."

For God, who said, "Let light shine out of darkness," made his light shine in our hearts to give us the light of the knowledge of the glory of God in the face of Christ.

But we have this treasure in jars of clay to show that this all-surpassing power is from God and not from us. We are hard pressed on every side, but not crushed; perplexed, but not in despair; persecuted, but not abandoned; struck down, but not destroyed....

Therefore we do not lose heart. Though outwardly we are wasting away, yet inwardly we are being renewed day by day. For our light and momentary troubles are achieving for us an eternal glory that far outweighs them all. So we fix our eyes not on what is seen, but on what is unseen. For what is seen is temporary, but what is unseen is eternal. (2 Corinthians 4:6–9, 16–18)

Unadorned clay pots. Vases with cracks. Earthenware jars with chips and dings and flaws. People with troubles, perplexities, weaknesses, traumas, and fear. That's all we are…without God.

But *with* God, oh we are so much more.

We are people with a treasure inside, and the value of the treasure is beyond price, reckoning, or comprehension. We are men and women with God's glory at work in us. His work doesn't entail removing our weaknesses or hardships. No, His work is displayed as He releases His divine power through our weaknesses.

When life is hard and God is in us...our broken places can become the windows where His glory shines through.

When life is hard and God is in us...we who are broken pots become trophies.

When life is hard and God is in us...we can rest assured that somehow, in some way, He will bring His redeeming value to bear in our lives. Good ol' Peter (who had a few dings and cracks of his own) summed it up nicely:

> Friends, when life gets really difficult, don't jump to the conclusion that God isn't on the job. Instead, be glad that you are in the very thick of what Christ experienced. This is a spiritual refining process, with glory just around the corner. (1 Peter 4:12, The Message)

The longer I work with trauma victims, the more I am convinced that there is *no* pain so deep or pervasive that God cannot heal, if a heart is open to Him. And as with Zena, the broken places of our lives—the fractures, fissures, and jagged edges—can become the very localities where God's glory spills through in a torrent of light, hope, and healing. Out of our own personal darkness, God's penetrating light may touch those who still grope in the shadows.

Just ask one of the regulars on the Rape Crisis Hotline.

Her voice is strong but softened by a deep compassion. The calls she receives on any given night vary wildly. But Zena knows her assignment. She knows she's supposed to be there...just for those who need a glimpse of a strong and steady light penetrating the long night.

CHAPTER THREE

WHEN YOU CAN'T HOLD IT TOGETHER

He existed before everything else began,
and he holds all creation together.
COLOSSIANS 1:17, NLT

I heard a story about a lady named Sandy who apparently likes to frequent Las Vegas.

During one of her recent visits, I was told, she was standing in front of a slot machine and noticed an elderly, white-haired lady on her left, yanking on that one-armed bandit as though her own bony arm was attached to it.

Suddenly Granny cashed in.

As lights flashed and bells clanged, shiny quarters began gushing down the chute—two-hundred-fifty-dollars worth, to be exact. The lady filled two buckets up to the rim with quarters. Then, rather than cashing in the coins for currency, she decided to haul the buckets back to her hotel suite. (She probably wanted to hear the delicious clink of coins as she ran her fingers through them.)

Sandy watched the Vegas Granny, hunched over from the mother lode, enter the elevator to go to her room. But it wasn't until the following day that Sandy heard the proverbial "rest of the story."

As usual, the elevator picked up others along the way. At the first stop, two large men stepped in and (all too conveniently, she thought) placed themselves behind her, on either side. Poor thing. Fear got the best of her, adrenaline kicked in, and her heart started pumping triple time...*ba-boom, ba-boom, ba-boom*.

The next thing she heard was an unmistakable command: "Hit the floor!"

In a panic, the old lady hit the floor face down, convinced she was about to meet her Maker.

After an exclamation of surprise, one of the gentlemen bent over and gently tapped her on the shoulder. "Ma'am," he said, "I'm really sorry we frightened you. I was talkin' to my friend. When I said, 'Hit the floor,' I meant, 'Hit the *hotel* floor.'" He pointed ruefully to the buttons on the elevator console.

When the elevator doors opened, that poor woman, shaken to the bone, couldn't crawl out fast enough! Just a little while later, hardly before she'd regained her composure, a knock on her door sent her adrenaline pumping all over again. Mustering courage, she croaked, "Who's there?"

A flower delivery man waited patiently until she finally cracked open the door for a peek. "Ma'am," he said, "I have a dozen red roses for you. Would you please take them?"

It seems Granny had hit the jackpot again. Each lovely rose was decorated with a shiny red bow. And inside each bow was a crisp, rolled-up hundred dollar bill. The enclosed note explained it all.

I'm so sorry we scared you.
Sincerely,
Eddie Murphy

Elevator experiences! We've all had them. Those moments when life catches us off guard and we leap to erroneous conclusions. Emotion overrides logic, and rather than pushing the button on the console, we do a face-plant on the elevator floor.

As with the little old lady in Vegas, when the unexpected happens, it's easy to assume the worst is yet to come.

A number of years ago I was locked in an elevator of sorts. And it was taking me where I didn't want to go. I had been invited to speak at a major women's conference but couldn't help wondering why God even had me there. Especially since He and I were in the middle of an intense power struggle.

Bottom line: I was pregnant, and I didn't *want* to be pregnant.

John and I were "finished having children," and it seemed to me that the Lord ought to be well aware of that fact. We already had a daughter, Jessie, and a son, Benjamin. With one child of each flavor, we were balanced. Content. Comfortable. It was "us four and no more," and we loved it that way. We loved our ministry. Life was working out very nicely.

Then, out of the blue, I turned up pregnant.

How could it be? Well, I knew how it *could* be, but it shouldn't have been! We'd taken all the precautions. Somehow this baby was conceived in spite of the foolproof birth-control method we'd used for the last seventeen years.

I guess we didn't have as much control as I thought we had. Life has a knack for teaching us that "control" is really an illusion.

At the time my emotions resembled a tossed salad: a wedge of guilt here, a slice or two of anger there, with some self-pity sprinkled over the top for spice. *Guilt*...because I had friends who wanted so very much to get pregnant and couldn't—and here I was upset and bitter that the little test stick had turned blue. *Anger*...because my agenda had been interrupted and rearranged. *Self-pity*...because I was sick all day every day through most of the pregnancy.

One morning during the conference I had some time off the platform, so I ordered breakfast in my room, read in the Gospel of John, and journaled my thoughts and feelings. I can assure you, God got an earful.

But then, after I'd vented, it was *His* turn.

There have been times through the years when the Lord has made something very clear to me, and this was one of those times. As I was reading in John 15, I came across two familiar verses that jolted me like a double dose of smelling salts. Jesus was speaking:

> "I am the true vine, and my Father is the gardener. He cuts off every branch in me that bears no fruit, while every branch that does bear fruit he prunes so that it will be even more fruitful." (John 15:1–2)

What I sensed God saying to me as I read those verses was, "Pam, you're not being set back; you're being *cut* back."

And in that instant a picture of the three rosebushes in our front yard came to mind. Each summer the bushes produce huge, yellow, long-stemmed roses that fill our home with glorious fragrance. Arranged in a vase on a table, the blooms seem to glow with a golden light of their own.

But in the fall, John cuts them back. *Way* back. After his pruning sheers do the job, I look at those stumps and think, "My goodness, the man is ruthless. Those poor things look decapitated!" Every fall I wonder if they'll ever grow back and…sure enough, every spring they do.

Pam, you're not being set back; you're being cut back.

In the quietness of that hotel room I knew God was up to something in my life—and that my pregnancy had in no way caught Him by surprise. For some incomprehensible reason, this was part of His plan to produce more beauty and fragrance in my life.

Ever so reluctantly I waved my little white flag. "Okay, Lord," I said. "If this is what You ask of me, I'll surrender to Your plan." That was no small first step! I wish I could say it had been easier for me.

How, then, do you and I "hold it together" when it feels like life is falling apart?

We surrender.

But not to "fate." Not to our emotions. Not to bitterness. No, we deliberately yield control to the One who holds all things together.

Oh yes, it all sounds nice enough—and spiritual to boot. But friend, surrender isn't always such a tidy bundle. Often it is a package seething with painful feelings like anger, rage, and deep sadness—which are *eventually* followed by release and peace. As we surrender, we experience our frustration and anger at God, at other people, at ourselves, and at life.

Oftentimes saying, "Yes Lord," simply opens the door to the grieving process. We suddenly find ourselves at the very core of our pain and sadness, the heavy emotional burden inside that has to be released before we can feel right again. By allowing ourselves to admit the grief through that front door of surrender, healing can slip in, quiet and unannounced, through the back door.

"Willpower" isn't the key...surrender is. For many years I've heard men and women from all walks of life say things like this:

- "I've invested too many years of my life trying to make people be what they don't want to be or do what they don't want to do. I've driven them—and myself—crazy in the process."
- "I spent my childhood trying to make an angry father

who didn't love himself be a normal person who loved me."

- "I've spent years trying to make emotionally unavailable people be emotionally present for me."
- "I've poured my life into trying to make unhappy family members happy, even though they don't seem interested in making the slightest effort."
- "I've given the last twenty-five years of my life, trying to make my alcoholic husband stop drinking."

What they are all saying in different words is something like this: *I have spent much of my life desperately and vainly trying to do the impossible and feeling like a dismal failure when I couldn't.* It's like planting carrot seeds and trying passionately, creatively, and desperately to make those little plants grow prize tomatoes— and feeling defeated when it doesn't work.

By surrendering, we gain the presence of mind to stop wasting time and energy trying to change and control that which we cannot change or control. Surrender gives us permission to stop trying to do the impossible and to focus on what *is* possible.

I wish I could say that surrender is a one-time event. It's not. Yielding to the Lord is a continual, daily, sometimes *hourly* process. God and I were in a wrestling match in that hotel room. Round One. But down the road (unbeknownst to me) were *many more* rounds to go.

Have you ever been in a wrestling match with God? Jacob was. Remember him? He was the first-class con man who lied to his blind, aged father and twice betrayed his only brother, eventually stealing Esau's very inheritance rights as the oldest son—the most precious thing the man possessed. The name Jacob means "crafty deceiver," and he tried hard to live up to his name.

Ah, but there came a night. Do you remember when this son of Isaac slipped through the ropes in the darkness and climbed into the ring with the Angel of the Lord?

> Jacob was left alone, and a man wrestled with him till daybreak. When the man saw that he could not overpower him, he touched the socket of Jacob's hip so that his hip was wrenched as he wrestled with the man. Then the man said, "Let me go for it is daybreak."
>
> But Jacob replied, "I will not let you go unless you bless me."
>
> The man asked him, "What is your name?"
>
> "Jacob," he answered.
>
> Then the man said, "Your name will no longer be Jacob, but Israel, because you have struggled with God and with men and have overcome."
>
> Jacob said, "Please tell me your name."
>
> But he replied, "Why do you ask my name?" Then he blessed him there.
>
> So Jacob called the place Peniel, saying, "It is because I saw God face to face, and yet my life was spared."
>
> The sun rose above him as he passed Peniel, and he was limping because of his hip. (Genesis 32:24–31)

The text says that God allowed Jacob to prevail—but before He let His man up off the mat, He also dislocated Jacob's hip. Let me assure you, friend, a dislocated hip isn't a hangnail or a bad hair day; it is an extremely painful condition. And through all the years of life that followed, it constantly reminded Jacob that he was not to depend on his own strength. He was to rely entirely on God.

God loves us so much that He *will* wrestle with us. He's not the "Burger King"; you're not going to "have it your way" all the time. That night when Jacob was alone in the dark, he wrestled with God...and God blessed his life. In spite of his seedy track record, in spite of his scheming, manipulative, and deceitful ways, God chose to open Heaven's great storehouses and pour His favor out upon Jacob. (Why does that encourage me so much?)

From that point on, Jacob knew his well-being was dependent on God's help, God's guidance, and God's blessing, not his own devices.

It's a lesson worth going to the mat for.

Or even the floor of an elevator.

CHAPTER FOUR

PROVISION

"I will answer them before they even call to me.
While they are still talking to me about their needs,
I will go ahead and answer their prayers!"
ISAIAH 65:24, NLT

John and I had just finished leading worship one Sunday and were moving towards our seats when a lady approached me, beckoned me to one side, and introduced herself.

"Hi," she whispered with a smile. "I'm Sugar."

I smiled back at this stranger and waited. What could she want? What was so important that she needed to speak to me in the middle of a church service?

"When you were singing, the Lord spoke to me," she said. "He told me I was to make myself available to help you."

I was a little taken aback. "Oh," I said cautiously, "in what way?"

She smiled again. "In whatever way you *need*...when the baby arrives."

I shook her hand, thanked her for her kindness, and found my seat. In all honesty I thought it was a little strange. *Why would I need help from a complete stranger when the baby comes? I've got John's help—and my mom will fly up to be with me.* We had it all planned.

Or so we thought.

Sugar and I ran into each other at church during the next

couple of months and made small talk. Then one day she called and asked if she could stop by to bring a gift for the baby. She stayed about thirty minutes and told me she lived just around the corner. As she spoke, she seemed strangely insistent.

"You call *anytime*," she told me, "day or night. I'm two minutes away, I'm awake at five every morning, and my kids are grown and gone. I can be here in a flash if you need anything." Again I thought it odd. It seemed very important to her that I got the message.

I didn't get it then...but I get it now.

Three and one-half months later John was hunting in eastern Oregon, and I was at a park with the kids—waddling around, feeling very pregnant. Toward the end of the day I felt extremely tired, and much to my surprise little jolts of pain shot through my belly. *No big deal,* I told myself. *I've just walked too much. I'll go home and go to bed. Everything will be fine.*

Oh, the power of denial!

By five the next morning my contractions were nine minutes apart. I kept thinking, *This CANNOT be happening! I have six more weeks to go. It has to be false labor.* (More denial.) But what was I going to do when the kids woke up?

Suddenly I remembered Sugar.

And just as she promised, she was at the front door in a flash. Sugar took charge of the house and tended to my needs while my neighbor Nancy pitched in to help with the children. Jessie and Ben went over to her house to play so that I could rest. Sugar and Nancy were gifts from the Father's hands to help me maintain my cool.

As the afternoon wore on, they kept saying, "Don't you think we'd better call John?" He was staying with a forest ranger in the middle of the boonies. I kept saying, "No, no, I don't want to ruin his hunting trip. I'll be fine."

Then my water broke. Sugar gave me one of those I'll-brook-no-more-argument looks and said, "It's time to call John!" She left a message with the ranger, who said he would try to find him.

Now you have to know a thing or two about John. He is a fanatic about hunting. Sunup on a hunting trip usually finds him perched in a tree stand, peering through the half-light for his game. And he stays on the hunt until there's barely enough light to see him back to camp. But on this particular afternoon, John had decided to pack it in early. He moseyed back to the ranger station around two in the afternoon and found a note tacked to the door: "YOUR WIFE IS IN LABOR!"

Within three minutes he'd tossed all his gear into the truck and was *blazing* a trail to Portland. The accelerator pedal never left the floor that day. He made a five-hour trip in half that time and told me afterward that angels must have been flying escort.

John dashed into the delivery room in his camouflage garb, green paint all over his face, just as Nathan's head was crowning. By now the drugs they'd given me were working marvelously well, and I was smiling through every contraction. Two minutes later, Nathan entered the world.

But something was wrong. Terribly wrong.

Our baby was blue, not breathing well, and his little cry sounded muted. Instead of laying him in my waiting arms, the technicians scurried around trying to suction his mouth to help him breathe. John held my hands and we prayed for Nathan, asking God to help him and to guide the doctors' efforts.

I kept asking the nurses if Nathan was all right, and all I could get out of them was, "He's in good hands, and they're helping clear his passageways." When I asked if I could nurse Nathan they said they didn't know. An hour later, impatient with vague answers and frustrated about being separated from my son, I asked the delivery nurse to wheel me into the care unit where they were working with Nathan. The pediatrician on call came over to talk with us. I didn't know this woman, and I didn't want to believe a word she was saying.

"Mrs. Vredevelt, your son is not oxygenating well, so we're trying to help him with oxygen and IVs."

"Is this life-threatening?" I asked.

"It could be," she replied. "It's also my observation that he has Down syndrome. I've called a cardiologist to examine him because I don't believe his heart is functioning properly."

At that point I wasn't tracking well and blurted out, "What does this mean?"

"It means he will be mentally retarded, Mrs. Vredevelt, and there is a higher incidence of leukemia for those with Down syndrome. There's a catheter in his heart, and the technicians are still working to stabilize him."

I spent that night alone in my room, listening to happy families around me celebrating their babies. My own personal doctor was in Russia. My pediatrician was on vacation. My parents were in California. John and the kids were home in bed, and a tiny little boy named Nathan Vredevelt was in some sterile room under impersonal fluorescent lights, fighting for his life.

And me? I began to wonder just how much God really loved me.

As hot tears rolled down my cheeks, I remember whispering into the night, "God, what is this? A bad joke? Well I'm not laughing!"

The next morning the cardiologist ran a battery of tests on Nathan. Based on the results, he said the center section of Nathan's heart was not formed and he would likely need open-heart surgery at four months. During surgery he would construct the center portions of Nathan's heart so that he could oxygenate better and follow a more normal growth pattern.

As the cardiologist left the room, wild and unchecked ruminations entered. *What if his heart fails and he doesn't make it four months? What if the surgery doesn't work? What if he gets sick and his body isn't strong enough to fight infection? How do we raise a child with Down syndrome? What if Jessie and Ben can't adjust to having a handicapped brother? What if…? What if…?*

While we were in the hospital, our pastor, Ted Roberts, asked the people at the Wednesday night church service to pray for Nathan. That very evening his vital signs took a turn for the better. His oxygenation improved, and by morning they were able to remove the IV that went directly into his heart. Four days later during the Sunday morning services, Ted asked the congregation to pray for Nathan again. This time they prayed specifically for the healing of his heart.

Mom flew into town to help us, and on the Tuesday following those Sunday services, she and I took Nathan to the hospital for more tests. The cardiologist wanted to examine all the cross sections of Nathan's heart on the ultrasound screen so he could determine how much of the heart muscle needed to be constructed.

We watched the screens intently as he focused on various chambers of the heart. When he got a clear shot of the center section, he started to shake his head and chuckle. Then in his clipped, British accent, he happily announced, "By golly, the center of his heart is absolutely normal!"

I started to cry, my mom started to cry, and the doctor just kept shaking his head in amazement, muttering, "Very good, oh, *very* good."

He pointed to a small hole between the upper and lower

chambers of the heart and showed on the screen where blood was spilling through. After taking some measurements, he consulted with us in his office.

"Mrs. Vredevelt," he said, "Nathan has two small holes in his heart. I want to watch these holes for the next six months and see if they will close on their own. If they do, surgery won't be necessary. If they don't close, then we'll need to patch them when he's a little older."

I cried again, Mom cried again, and the doctor beamed broadly, telling us how much he enjoyed giving good news.

I left the hospital that day with a renewed awareness: God was still in the business of healing. That truth applied to baby boys with holes in their hearts, and grown-up mommies with holes in their faith.

Either way, His is the touch that heals.

CHAPTER FIVE

A Child
Among Them

*At that time Jesus said, "I praise you, Father,
Lord of heaven and earth, because you have hidden
these things from the wise and learned,
and revealed them to little children."*
MATTHEW 11:25

For the two young adults standing at the altar, it was a dream come true.

For their parents, it was a miracle akin to waltzing on water.

It looked for all the world like a typical wedding. But there wasn't anything typical about it. As the bride and groom said, "I do," every handkerchief and Kleenex in the building was getting a royal workout. Everyone knew the long, hard road this young man and young woman had traveled to stand side by side in front of the pastor that day.

Both bride and groom were autistic.

To appreciate the dimensions of this miracle you have to understand a bit of what that means.

Autism is a neurological disorder that begins in infancy or early childhood. Those who suffer with the condition range widely in their degree of functioning. Some are affected in a mild way, others more severely. Children with severe autism withdraw from the world into a dreamlike existence. Most attempts to bring them out of their fantasy are usually met with fear and anxiety. Social relationships are impaired because the autistic child has little awareness of the existence or feelings of others, and prefers to play alone. When autism is severe, there is rarely babbling, facial expressions, gestures, mimes, or spoken language. Even if the child does speak, it's unlikely he will initiate or sustain a conversation with others. Instead, he tends to indulge in lengthy monologues and repetitive phrases on one subject, regardless of interjections from others.

Lynn, the mother of the bride, told me all about it recently.

"Parenting an autistic child was no easy assignment," she sighed. "From the time DeeDee was born, she was tactile defensive. She didn't allow me to hug or hold her without throwing fits. She was like a wary, caged animal poised to strike at anything that entered her space. It was hard having a toddler who shoved me away. I couldn't help but envy other moms whose children crawled up their legs, begging to be carried and held."

A slight smile brightened her face as she reflected.

"But sometimes it worked to my advantage. If DeeDee wasn't cooperative, all I had to do was threaten to *hug* her and immediately she obeyed! She hated any kind of touch. The threat worked every time except once. I'll never forget that day…" Her voice trailed off as she glanced away.

"What day?" I prompted.

Tears filled her eyes when she turned to answer me.

"It happened when I was the 'old me.' I used to be the lead singer in a rock band—and a drug dealer besides. Unlike the rest of my buddies, I got caught. Part of my penalty was community service. The authorities assigned me to support-group meetings for parents with special needs children. I went along with the system to develop a good-girl image as a front for my dark side deals. It worked. The leaders of the group saw promise in me…and made me an instructor!

"DeeDee came with me to the weekly meetings. I was constantly afraid she would blow my image, so I threatened to hold her if she didn't sit still in the chair. At the time DeeDee was six years old and had never spoken. Not one word. But when she was bothered, everyone knew it. She was a master at acting out her frustrations. After threatening her, she performed like a perfect angel at the meetings...except on this particular afternoon.

"I'd been invited to give the keynote address at a Parents with Special Needs Children luncheon. I told them my story of raising DeeDee alone as a single parent, with no friends or family to help. Everyone had deserted me when DeeDee was an infant—they couldn't stand her screaming. Nothing made her happy! My family and friends couldn't deal with it, so they left. I tried to convince the parents in the audience that if *I* could do this completely alone, then they could, too.

"My topic for the luncheon was 'Ten Steps to Successfully Parenting an Autistic Child.'" Lynn grinned at me. "Sounds great, huh? It wasn't. It was a bunch of self-help fluff. But it served as a really good cover for my...extracurricular activities.

"There I was, spouting off about what to do and what not to do when DeeDee suddenly got up out of her seat, walked onto the stage, stood behind the podium, and began to mimic me.

"Pam, it was *really* strange—because autistic children don't mimic. Standing on her tiptoes, she picked up my papers and straightened them into a nice neat stack. The audience was spellbound. I broke into a cold sweat not knowing what was coming next.

"DeeDee reached for the gooseneck microphone attached to the podium, pulled it down to her mouth, and with perfect clarity spoke her very first words:

"*You're never alone if you have Jesus.*'

"The audience burst into thunderous applause. I turned green and felt like I was going to lose my lunch. Where had she learned such nonsense? She'd never heard those words from me! I promptly excused both of us from the platform, saying DeeDee was ill and we needed to leave.

"On the way home I stopped at a park for some fresh air, trying to make sense out of what had just happened. I was so blown away. As I sat in the grass rehearsing the last hour, DeeDee approached me, looked me in the eye, and said:

"'Did you know Jesus can take a black heart and make it as white as snow?'

"'Did you know that Jesus can make your life new again?'

"'Did you know you are never alone if you have Jesus?'

"Like a broken record, she repeated those three phrases over and over again. The repetition I recognized as part of the autism. But the message seemed to come from another planet. I was so angry—and determined to find out who was brain-washing my child!

"My mother usually took DeeDee to a little country church on Sunday mornings so that I could sleep in after performing at bars into the wee hours. I didn't know anything about the place but figured they were teaching her to chant some kind of mantras. How else would she have learned those phrases so well?

"The following Sunday I dressed in my battle gear and took DeeDee to church, determined to put an end to their influence. Decked in forty pounds of turquoise jewelry, jeans slit clear up the side, and my long hair frizzed out like a lion's mane, I stormed into church ready to set some people straight.

"There were about sixty people there, all over the age of fifty. I'd chosen my garb carefully to intimidate them. Instead, their love scared *me*. When we walked in the door, we were quickly surrounded by smiling faces and open arms and invited to sit in the front row. What was happening? Nothing made sense to me. Why would complete strangers love me and my daughter, when our own flesh and blood didn't?

"When the music started, DeeDee rocked from side to side and clapped her hands. She was used to the bar crowd who moved with the beat. The people around us were very conservative and sat perfectly still but turned and nodded our way, grinning with approval.

"I sat in the pew that morning and silently seethed. After all, God had never done anything for *me*. I drove an old clunker car, when all of my friends owned spiffy sports cars. I got caught dealing; they didn't. They all had perfect babies; mine had defects. After fifteen minutes I'd had enough church and stood up to leave.

"But DeeDee grabbed my hand.

"That alone was significant, because she had never purposely reached out to touch me since the day she was born. When DeeDee took my hand, it was as if something hit me. I fell to the floor and began to weep. Four older ladies quietly knelt beside me and prayed. DeeDee sat with me, calmly holding my hand as though she'd done it every day of her life."

Lynn closed her eyes as the memory swept over her again.

"Pam, it was like a blanket of love, peace, and joy embraced every inch of me. No drug can give you that kind of a trip! As I lay there on the floor, I knew *God* was with me. I told Him I didn't care about having fancy cars or impressive stuff. I—I just wanted what He'd given DeeDee. That would be enough.

"I didn't understand what happened to me in that little country church, but I saw the world very differently from that point forward. It was as if blinders had been lifted from my eyes. I went home that afternoon, and my four-year-old son smiled up at me from the kitchen table. He was rolling joints. That was his way of helping out when we were dealers. Walking into that kitchen was like walking into a fiery furnace. I was blasted with an acute awareness that all of this was very wrong.

"That Sunday night our band was scheduled to audition for a major gig in town. I went, even though I didn't want to go. But I still wasn't sure *why* I didn't want to go.

"During the audition someone turned on the lights in the bar, even though no one flipped a switch. I saw things I'd never seen before. The men hitting on the women. The drug deals going down backstage, destroying innocent lives. The drinking. The swearing. The filth. The darkness.

"At the end of the audition the manager told us we had the job if we wanted it. The guys in the band turned to me and said, 'How about it?' All I could say was, 'I can't sing anymore unless it's for God.'

"They all split a gut laughing. Said it was the best joke they'd heard in a long time. But I wasn't joking. And I didn't take the job.

"A week later DeeDee and I were invited to another church meeting to hear some special guest speakers. As I listened to them talk, I realized God had touched my life in that little country church and that He loved me. The speakers invited everyone who wanted all God had to offer to come forward for prayer. I went, and some friendly women met me at the end of the aisle and began to pray with me. As I basked in the warmth of that moment, some unfamiliar words passed through my mind: *'I will restore what the locust has eaten.'*

"Before we left that night I asked one of the ladies in the church about woodworms. I hadn't heard the word before and didn't know what it meant. She smiled, opened her King James

Bible and showed me a verse she called Joel 2:25: 'And I will restore to you the years that the locust hath eaten....'

"As I heard those words, I understood that God was going to change everything I hated about my life. I didn't know how or why, but I knew without a doubt it would happen.

"That was sixteen years ago. And God kept His promise. A month later my husband opened his heart to God, and within a year the entire rock band abandoned the darkness for the light. I continued to teach parents about raising autistic children, but the message changed. They heard about a mom whose black heart was washed white as snow. They heard about a lonely parent whom God sought out. They heard about a mom who is never alone in the struggle. And they heard that God wanted to help them, too. They only had to ask."

Lynn and DeeDee's story is still in progress, but to date Lynn has had the privilege of praying with hundreds of parents with autistic children. Over thirty moms and dads have responded to her challenge and, for the first time in their lives, have asked God for help. They too have discovered a God who loves them in a deep and personal way.

And it all started with a little girl called out of a silent, broken world by the tender words of Jesus.

This is the same Jesus who held a little child to His chest and said, "I tell you the truth, unless you change and become like little children, you will never enter the kingdom of heaven. Therefore, whoever humbles himself like this child is the greatest in the kingdom of heaven" (Matthew 18:3–4).

What was Jesus saying to His disciples in the olive orchard that day? What is He saying to you and me today?

He's saying we need to change. We need to become like the little girl who quickly believed God could take a black heart and wash it white as snow. We need to heed the message of a handicapped six-year-old who told her bar-hopping mom: "Did you know, God can take your life and make it brand new?" And, "When you have Jesus in your heart you are never alone."

We need to realize that jewelry, spiffy cars, fancy things, and prestigious positions of power don't make us great. Only God at work in a humble heart can do that.

Where self-sufficiency falters and fails, God is just getting warmed up.

That thought may have crossed DeeDee's mind as she and her groom walked down the aisle that afternoon and into a new life. Then again, she probably knew it all along.

CHAPTER SIX

WHAT MY FATHER HAD IN MIND

You have turned my mourning
into joyful dancing.
You have taken away my clothes of mourning
and clothed me with joy.
PSALM 30:11, NLT

After Nathan came home from the hospital, I struggled with depression, driven by postpartum hormones, anxiety about the holes in my baby's heart, and my inability to meet the needs of Jessie and Ben as I had before.

Two months after Nathan was born, I stood in the shower, telling God all about it.

"I am so *sick* of crying, God. I've cried every day for the last two months, and I'm SICK of it. I can't fix me. I can't fix my family. I can't fix Nathan. God…I need help. Your Word says You can turn mourning into joy. God, would You please do that for me? Because—no matter how hard I try—I can't do it myself."

I call that ten minute episode "Surrender in the Shower." It was a turning point for me.

—I surrendered to the fact that I was powerless to change Nathan's condition. I couldn't rewrite the script, nor could I erase the last year of my life.

—I surrendered to the fact that I wasn't capable of meeting my children's needs the way I wanted to. God knew that, too, and He was going to have to make up the difference.

—I surrendered to the fact that I couldn't control the future. It was in God's hands.

—And I surrendered to the fact that my feelings were my feelings—even though I hated them—and the only way to get beyond the grief was to go *through* it and to trust that in God's perfect time He would heal my heart.

Two weeks later I flew down to California with Nathan, to rest and be with my parents. On those visits I love to take walks with my dad. He is a great friend and mentor to me. One morning he wasn't able to walk due to an early appointment at the office, so I went on alone.

It was a dark November day, and the gloomy weather matched my mood precisely. As I turned a corner, I saw this stumpy treelike thing planted in the middle of someone's front yard. It was about a foot in diameter, five feet high, and had short, ugly, foot-long nubs pointing in every direction on top. It was gray, grotesque, and looked absolutely pitiful. The words came back again.

"You're not being set back, Pam. You are being cut back."

As I looked at that pathetic stump, I started to cry. Hanging on to a streetlight post for support, I blubbered, "That's me! Right there, that thing's me. A dead old stump. No life. No color. No beauty. A pruned-back unsightly mess!"

Now when you start hugging lampposts in broad daylight, you know you're really in trouble! When I got home, my dad met me at the door. If he noticed I'd been crying (and how could he help it?), he said nothing about it.

"I'd like you to set aside a couple of hours for me this afternoon," he said. He didn't say why. He simply asked me to be ready by two because he wanted to take me somewhere. Curiosity got the best of me and sent my mind into the investigation mode, trying to figure out what dad had planned.

I concluded it had something to do with grave plots.

Just the day before, Mom and Dad had told me they'd been discussing the phone calls they were getting from solicitors for buying burial plots. In my dismal state of mind, I gathered that Dad was going to take me out to some cemetery to show me potential grave sites. *Great*, I thought, *he's going to take the walking dead to see where she'll bury her dead parents. Won't this be a lark!*

When Dad walked out of his bedroom at two o'clock sharp, however, he was decked out in a sport coat, tie, and nice slacks. That seemed a little odd, but I figured the cemetery must be a first-class act. Something in the high rent district. We drove through town, talking about this and that, and twenty minutes later Dad pulled into a parking lot.

But this wasn't a cemetery, it was *Nordstrom!*

Startled I said, "What—are we doing here?"

With a twinkle in his eye, Dad told me that he and Mom wanted to buy me a new coat and purse.

My eyes widened to the size of quarters—and I suddenly felt...*energized!* Shopping! Now that was more like it. After trying on dozens of coats, I found one I really liked and asked Dad to hold it for me. But just then the saleslady appeared from the back room with yet another coat and said, "You should try this one on, too. It came in just today."

When I slipped it over my shoulders, I heard Dad say quietly, "That looks really nice." Turning to the saleslady, he said, "We'll take them both."

I tried to argue—a little—but he was determined. He won.

With coats in hand we were off to the purse department. I headed straight for the bargain table, but Dad went around the corner and started talking with another saleslady. I picked out a couple of purses that were between $50 and $60 and took them to show Dad.

"Pam," he said, "we wanted to buy you a purse like I bought your mother last Christmas, but they don't sell them here anymore. This lady says these purses are just as nice. Do you like any of them?"

Sharp saleslady. She could tell from the bargain purses I'd selected that I wanted plain black, with a shoulder strap, handles, and lots of room. So she plunked a beautiful purse down in front of me and said, "How's this?"

Well, it was perfect. Top quality leather. Beautifully made. Roomy. Black. And I also noticed it had an insignia on it. Not being a connoisseur of purses, I didn't know who Dooney and Bourke were—nor did I know how much they charged for their purses. So without thinking, I said, "It's perfect. How much is it?" When she told me, I nearly passed out on the floor. That saleslady was obviously used to working with much higher class customers; she couldn't seem to identify with my sticker shock.

Dad and I spent an hour in Nordstrom that day, and I left with two new coats, a Dooney and Bourke purse, and a lesson I'll never forget.

When Dad and I set out on our excursion, I was anticipating the worst. You know you're in a bit of a funk when your fantasies are filled with tombstones. All my fears and anxieties were distorting my perception. Wow, was I wrong. What my father had in mind for me and what I *thought* he had in mind for me were worlds apart. It never crossed my mind that a special surprise awaited around the corner.

That night when I went to bed, a Scripture came to mind that I had memorized years before in Bible college. Jesus was talking to His disciples when He said:

"I say to you: Ask and it will be given to you; seek and you will find; knock and the door will be opened to you. For everyone who asks receives; he who seeks finds; and to him who knocks, the door will be opened.

"Which of you fathers, if your son asks for a fish, will give him a snake instead? Or if he asks for an egg, will give him a scorpion? If you then, though you are evil, know how to give good gifts to your children, how much more will your Father in heaven give the Holy Spirit to those who ask him!" (Luke 11:9–13)

God used my trip to Nordstrom with Dad to teach me something very important. *What He had in mind for our family's future and what I had in mind were worlds apart.* He wanted me to know there were wonderful surprises ahead…if I would only trust Him.

I'd been thinking of pruned-back stumps, dead ends, and tombstones. My Father was thinking fresh roses, two new coats, and Dooney and Bourke.

His surprises had only begun.

CHAPTER SEVEN

ANGEL BEHIND THE ROCKING CHAIR

"See that you do not look down on one of these little ones.
For I tell you that their angels in heaven
always see the face of my Father in heaven."
MATTHEW 18:10

From the day we brought him home from the hospital, Nathan and I have had a bedtime ritual.

We nestle together in a big stuffed rocking chair, and I sing praise songs while rocking him. He lies in my arms, his eyes fixed on mine, until the picture blurs and he drifts off to sleep.

One night when Nathan was eighteen months old, I was feeding him a bottle of milk during our nightly routine. But rather than looking at me—as he had every other night—he kept turning his head toward the blank wall on the opposite side of the nursery. It was dark, and for the life of me I couldn't see anything there to distract him and hold his attention.

Each time he turned away his mouth lost suction, and milk ran down his cheek onto me. Wanting to fill his belly and keep my pants dry, I tried turning his head toward me for the fourth time. It was no use. His sights were *locked* onto something on that wall. But there was nothing there. No shadows, no pattern of light. Nothing.

By then I was becoming curious. "Nathan," I said softly, "do you see something? What do you see?"

Dumb question. Even if he had been able to reply verbally

(which was not yet in his ability range), I was plugging his mouth with a bottle! I'm not sure what prompted me, but I turned his head toward me again and said, "Nathan, do you see *angels?*"

I still don't know why I asked that question, because angels weren't a topic of conversation in our home. We didn't even have any children's books with angel pictures. But when I used that word, I feel quite sure that Nathan understood.

He riveted his attention back on the blank wall and smiled from ear to ear. It was as if he were saying, "Way to go, Mom. You finally got it."

I hid that incident in my heart and nearly forgot about it until Nathan was three. The scene was much the same. Same rocker. Same time of evening. Same nightly ritual. But rather than lying in my arms, this time he tucked his knees up in my lap and rested his head on my shoulder while I sang. When we were both nearly asleep, he bolted straight back, bounced up and down, and pointed wildly behind the rocker, shouting, "Aaa! Aaa! Aaa!"

Impatient with his antics, I retorted, "Nathan, it is not time to play! It's time to go to sleep!"

But he kept bouncing, pointing behind the chair, and shouting, "Aaa! Aaa! AAA!" His persistence suddenly reminded me of that earlier time when he'd stared and smiled at the wall.

"Nathan," I asked, "do you see angels?"

This time he added "Da!" to his smile, put his head back down, and promptly fell asleep. "Da" in Nathan's vocabulary means "yes."

Being a doubting Thomas, I ran a test the next morning. When our friend Margaret came to the house, I said, "Nathan, can you show Margaret where you saw the angels last night?"

He took her by the hand, marched her into the nursery, and

pointed behind the rocker. I'm no longer a skeptic.

In his letter to the Corinthians, Paul wrote:

> We have not received the spirit of the world but the Spirit who is from God, that we may understand what God has freely given us. This is what we speak, not in words taught us by human wisdom but in words taught by the Spirit. (1 Corinthians 2:12–13)

I guess Nathan's vocabulary was broader than we thought; we hadn't taught him the word "angel." He must have learned it from his Other Teacher…the One who instructs him in the ways of the Spirit.

AT THE
PETTING ZOO

And hope does not disappoint us,
because God has poured out his love
into our hearts by the Holy Spirit,
whom he has given us.
ROMANS 5:5

Some gifts come in large packages, others small. It really doesn't matter much to me, just so long as I get a few of 'em! I love surprises.

One Christmas our family decided to do something different. Rather than exchange gifts, we went on a four-day trip to Disneyland. The whole crew hopped a plane and then bus after bus to stand in line after line at "the happiest place on earth." At least that's what the man on TV called it.

And boy, did we party. We ran from one ride to the next, hitting any hot dog, cotton candy, or popcorn stand in our path. (There oughta be a law against charging a family over thirty bucks for five hot dogs and lemonade!) By the end of the first day our pockets were empty and we were drop-dead tired.

But hey, this was Christmas, and there was no stopping us. Seven in the morning rolled around, and Jessie and Ben were shaking us, saying, "C'mon, Mom 'n' Dad, let's beat the lines!" With our stomachs full of pancakes, we launched our second day. (By the fourth day we were all comatose and didn't care *who* beat us to the park.)

By 2:00 P.M. the lines for the attractions ran together in one big mass; someone said there were 80,000 in the park that day. I believe it! Nathan was fussing in the stroller, and we weren't sure what was wrong. His Down syndrome didn't allow him to form words like other three-year-olds, so we had to work a little harder to figure out his needs.

As we strolled along, I couldn't help noticing other little ones with their parents. They chattered in complete sentences and seemed more aware of what was going on around them.

In spite of myself, I felt a haze of sadness descending.

Doggone it, I thought, *here I am feeling sad smack dab in the middle of "the happiest place on earth"! Lord, this is no place or time for grief therapy.* Turning my face from the rest of my family, I brushed away the tears.

The next thing I heard John say was, "Hey, there's a petting zoo. Let's show the kids the animals."

Released from his stroller, Nathan was like a heat-seeking missile, his sights locked onto a huge sheep resting under a shade tree. He moved as fast as his little legs could carry him and did a sprawling belly flop right on top of that poor animal. That's about the time we figured that old Walt was slipping the sheep Valium, because that blob of wool didn't so much as flinch.

While Nathan clutched the big ewe like a long lost teddy bear, Jessie and Ben went exploring around the little zoo. I looked up for a moment and noticed someone on the far side of the neatly fenced courtyard. She was blonde, walked with an irregular gait, and had eyes shaped like Nathan's. Another child with Down syndrome—maybe ten or eleven years old. I made a beeline toward her.

As I drew near, I saw her eyeball to eyeball with a couple of attentive little goats, and she was talking a blue streak. "Wow!"

I blurted out, "she can *talk!*" Then I immediately looked around, hoping no one had heard me.

I watched her for a long time, finding comfort in the affectionate words and laughter she poured into the ears of those wiry little critters. They had something going with her! Whenever she started walking away, they scampered in front of her and nudged her with their noses for a few more strokes. In the next few minutes I learned that goats have the power to discriminate. When I leaned over to scratch their backs, all *I* got were their indifferent hindquarters in my face.

They weren't interested in being patronized. They wanted authentic love. And that little girl was pouring it over them in a melodic stream.

When I saw the girl's parents walk up, I introduced myself. "Hi, I'm Pam from Portland. I got the biggest kick out of hearing your daughter talk with the animals." They laughed and told me all about her heart surgeries and nine years of speech therapy. I pointed to Nathan and for a couple of minutes shared the joys and challenges he had added to our family. They nodded and smiled, and with a surge of warmth, I knew they weren't merely being polite. They really *understood.* They just happened to be seven years ahead of us on the path.

Then that kind father, probably ten years my senior, looked me straight in the eye. With a little shake of his head and a blinding smile, he said something I will never forget.

"Oh," he said, "you have *so much* to look forward to."

That was the best Christmas present I received that year. A little nine-word sentence, wrapped in love and ribboned with hope. A special Christmas package from my Heavenly Father, sent special delivery by a little girl with Down syndrome and her parents—who "just happened" to bump into us in the midst of 80,000 others at Disneyland.

Coincidence? I don't think so!

God's answer to the prayer I had murmured through my tears just moments before? You'd better believe it.

God has a way of breathing fresh hope into weary souls in ways we least expect. All it takes is a whispered prayer, a simple cry for help in all the confusion, and an open heart when we feel life closing in like a vise. It doesn't take trying harder; it takes trust. The same truths Paul taught the Romans he passes on to all-American amusement park vacationers:

> May the God of hope fill you with all joy and peace as you trust in him, so that you may overflow with hope by the power of the Holy Spirit. (Romans 15:13)

I brushed away a few more tears that afternoon, but the sadness had lifted, like clouds dispersed by a freshening wind. In its place was a renewed sense of trust in my Heavenly Father's tender care. My groans had turned into giggles, especially when I tried to peel Nathan off the patient ewe we'd nicknamed Two-Ton Tess. He had such a death grip around her neck I thought we were going to have to shear her to separate those two. Nathan could *not* understand why Tess couldn't come home with us. So we distracted him with a bribe he couldn't resist: the promise of another five-dollar hot dog and lemonade.

Hope put a smile on his face, too.

CHAPTER NINE

THE LEGACY OF FAITH CHRISTINA

Some day I will go to him, but he cannot come back to me."
2 SAMUEL 12:23, NCV

Kim began the day with a heavy heart.

Her father had been diagnosed with inoperable lung cancer two weeks before. She was hoping for some support from her obstetrician when she saw him that afternoon. Sure enough, Dr. Sargent listened patiently and offered words of comfort.

She shared her fears of losing her father and the suffering he would endure. Her father's cancer overshadowed the other concerns she carried into the appointment, five months pregnant. The scales said she had lost two pounds since the last visit, and Kim told Dr. Sargent that the baby seemed quiet.

An ultrasound test confirmed the sad news.

Kim's baby did not have a heartbeat. She was told she would need to go to the hospital the next day to be induced for delivery.

Kim sat on the end of the examining table and cried and prayed. With her hands raised to the Lord, she said, "God, I surrender myself to You. I know You are good—even though this feels like more sadness than I can bear. Why, God? *Why did this have to happen?*"

By 1:38 P.M. the following day, the delivery was complete, and the doctor told Kim and Joe they had a little girl. They were relieved, knowing the ordeal was over. The nurses wrapped the baby in blankets and handed her to Joe and Kim.

She stayed with them all night.

Kim rocked her and prayed and thanked God for the precious time they were able to have with their daughter before saying good-bye.

Kim and Joe talked of names, and "Faith Christina" seemed to fit the best. Only through their faith in Christ could they bear the pain they felt that night. Only faith in Him could sustain them in the double loss of the baby and Kim's dad.

Pastor Warren visited the family in the hospital room and read the story about King David's sick baby, who died a few hours after birth. David said, "Can I bring him back again? I will go to him, but he will not return to me" (2 Samuel 12:23). As the early morning hours passed, Kim rocked Faith Christina and spoke to her of things stored in a mother's heart. Strength came from knowing Faith Christina had moved beyond the hands of time into the hands of God. Kim and Joe looked forward to the day when they would be reunited as a family.

Family and friends gathered at Faith Christina's memorial service to offer support and comfort to Kim and Joe and their three-year-old son, Andrew. Kim's father, battling pain from his chemotherapy, was unable to attend.

He wasn't a man of many words. At the time he wasn't a church-going person either and didn't often speak his heart. But he apologized for his absence and told Kim, "I love you."

Kim and Joe brought a tape recorder to make a copy of the memorial service for him. The pastors created a series of beautiful reflections that comforted and encouraged all who attended.

But yet another disappointment followed.

After the service Kim and Joe realized they hadn't turned on the built-in microphone switch. Nothing had been recorded. The tape was blank.

Pastor Warren heard of the mishap and offered to visit Kim's father at home and informally share the memorial service with him. Kim was excited about the proposition, but what would her dad say? He wasn't used to preachers being in his home.

A few days later the pastor called Kim with the news that the deacon board was praying for her dad. Mustering up the courage, she asked her dad if he would be willing to hear the message of Faith's memorial service from Pastor Warren at home.

Much to her surprise, he said, "Sure!"

A week later the pastor joined Kim at her parents' home and delivered the same message he had at Faith's service. Kim's mom and dad were attentive, and Pastor Warren was loving and straightforward. He asked Kim's father if he knew Jesus Christ. The man's answers, however, were vague and indirect. To him, religion was strictly a private affair.

Ten days later Kim was watching the five o'clock news on TV and saw a moving story about a man who was running in the Mount Hood-to-the-Coast Relay in honor of his late brother. At the end of the story, the man said he'd learned an important lesson from losing his brother. He looked into the camera and said, *"Don't put off to tomorrow what you can do today. Spend time with your family while you have them!"*

It was as though he was speaking directly to Kim. Immediately she picked up the phone and dialed her dad, asking if she could come see him. She visited most every day, but on this particular evening she'd planned to stay home. Her dad said he was tired, but if she wanted to come, he would stay up awhile. When she arrived, her brother and sister happened to drop in, too. They ordered pizza and had a nice evening as a family, laughing over a silly television show together.

Around nine o'clock, however, Kim's dad was suddenly

unable to breathe. Someone dialed 9–1–1, and the paramedics arrived within minutes. Kim's dad waved good-bye to them from the back of the ambulance as he was driven away.

Pastor Warren met the family at the hospital. Kim's dad was transferred from the emergency room to intensive care. Visitation was limited to two at a time in five-minute increments. Kim and Pastor Warren joined her dad at his bedside. He was unable to speak due to the tubes in his mouth and difficulty breathing...but he wanted the pastor to stay.

When Pastor Warren asked if he would like him to pray, the stricken man nodded yes. During part of the prayer, the pastor quoted Romans 10:13: "Whoever will call upon the name of the Lord will be saved."

By 6:00 the next morning Kim's dad's heart rate dropped— and the heart monitor went flat. He was gone. When she left his room and walked the hospital corridors, Kim was truly hopeful that her dad was getting acquainted with another new arrival in heaven...Faith Christina.

In a conversation a few days later, one of Kim's friends expressed the same thought. She said, "Maybe your dad's in heaven bouncing Faith Christina on his knee!"

Some say a baby in the womb isn't worth much. Just a throwaway lump of tissue. Kim and Joe disagree. They believe their little girl was responsible for Kim's dad meeting Jesus...and walking through the gates of eternal life. Had it not been for Faith Christina, her dad wouldn't have heard about God's love in terms that were relevant to him. But a tiny package in pink who visited this world for a brief five months touched her grandfather's heart. And an "off" switch on a tape recorder brought a faithful servant of Christ to his door to deliver a message in person. The privacy of that pastor's home visit gave Kim's dad the courage to nod yes to a prayer in ICU, just hours before his life was complete.

No, there is no question in Kim's and Joe's minds that God took a terrible double loss...and turned it into eternal gain. The pain still hasn't gone away, and likely never will completely. But their loss is tempered with hope.

And when the whispering "if only's" creep in (as they inevitably do), this dear couple try their best not to pay attention. They choose to focus on the *unseen* rather than the *seen*. They choose to believe.

They believe little Faith Christina was on a mission. Her brief life had eternal purpose. She made her mark on this world...and she also made her mark in the world to come.

Something inside tells Kim and Joe that their little girl's "mark" is her Grandpa's name, written in the Lamb's Book of Life.

Just in time.

ॐ

Postscript: On June 25, 1997, Kim and Joe welcomed Jonathan Michael into their family. After a five-hour labor, Mom and seven-pound-thirteen-ounce baby are healthy and fine. Faith Christina has a second brother.

CHAPTER TEN

WANDERINGS

You number my wanderings;
Put my tears into Your bottle;
Are they not in Your book?
PSALM 56:8, NKJV

John and I had always thought Down syndrome meant "slow."

Ummm. Not always.

Sometimes we joke about Nathan being our unguided missile. When he was two years old, he rocketed through every room in the house in three minutes, turning our moderately tidy home into a demolition zone.

Salt and pepper shakers clunked their way down the laundry chute. The kitchen wastebasket became his basketball hoop for slam dunking Mom's jewelry, Dad's slippers, Jessie's baby dolls, and Ben's hot rod remote. As luck would have it, we usually discovered these treasures buried under a foot of wrappers, coffee grinds, and whatever else had been pitched.

Then came that new Olympic event: The Pantry Climb.

We have a large pantry in our kitchen, seven shelves high. Nathan learned to scale it in six seconds flat. Trouble was, once he got *up*, he had no idea how to get *down*. After a while I began to recognize "the cry from the pantry." It was a frantic "Mamamamamaaaaaa!" Each time I heard that distinctive SOS, I dropped everything, ran to the kitchen, and found him clinging for dear life to the woodwork. I peeled him off the shelf for the last time after he had dumped a huge sack of oats and sent the mobile contents of an economy-sized box of Cheerios rolling across 100 square feet of kitchen floor.

But if he thought the kitchen was fun 'n' games, bathrooms were better yet.

I'm not a handyman, so John—after long days at the office—bore the brunt of the unique plumbing challenges. I've lost count of the times he's had to arm himself with plumber's snake and plunger in order to unclog the sink and toilet. Nathan has been known to shove all the family toothbrushes down the sink drain. He must have thought toilet flushing was a magic trick, because we roto-rootered golf balls, hair brushes, baby bottles, socks, toys, and Barbie doll heads out of our plumbing. (Imagine what Freud would do with that one!)

On several occasions we had to send Ben, who was five at the time, outside to tinkle in the bushes because our toilets were out of commission. We could just imagine what the neighbors were saying: "There goes that pastor's kid again, fertilizin' the bushes. You'd *think* his father would teach him some manners, wouldn't ya? What's the name of their church again? East Something? Heaven only knows what they teach their people there."

After five months of flushing, the novelty wore off, and Nathan went on to more advanced missions. If toys, bottles, and Barbie heads could perform disappearing acts, why couldn't he?

That's when John started referring to him as "our little escape artist." The now-you-see-me-now-you-don't game started in the church nursery. In the blink of an eye, Nathan bolted out of class and blitzed down the aisle toward the front of the worship center. Pastor Ted was at a serious point in the middle of his sermon when hundreds of heads turned in unison to witness a grown woman in a skirt sprint down the center aisle and swoop Nathan up in her arms just before he tagged the platform.

Pastor Ted didn't miss a beat. He finished his sentence, smiled at the lady, and said, "Nice catch, Mom." Feeling my face get hot, I said to myself, *That's right—it's HER son, not ours!*

I didn't get off as easy the next time. I was standing at my kitchen sink loading the dishwasher when Norene, the neighborhood grandma, appeared at my door with Nathan in tow.

"Nathan walked into our house and crawled behind the rocking chair," she told me with a smile. "I think he wanted to play with the cats."

I landed somewhere between shocked and mortified.

Without my knowing it, Nathan had walked barefoot up the hill and into Art and Norene's house. Scarcely two minutes before, I was with him in the bathroom brushing his teeth. When I thought he was in his room playing quietly with toys, he was actually making himself comfortable in someone else's den. *Now* what did the neighbors think?

After a stern talk with Nathan, I had high hopes he wouldn't pull that particular shenanigan again. After all, our reputation was at stake. I doubt he understood the word *reputation,* but he did sense Mommy wasn't happy.

The wandering, however, continued unabated.

Sometimes it happened in the middle of the night. In those dark hours of early morning, I'd surface from the depths of slumber to hear a little voice yelling "Maaaaaa-Maaaaaaaaaaaaaaaa!" from somewhere other than a bedroom. I would grope and stumble my way out to the living room or kitchen and find him standing in the dark, wondering where he was and how he got there.

Then there were times when Anna, the little girl three houses up the street, brought him home. Next it was her brother

Trent, followed by their mom, Nancy. Dennis next door, and Tony and Luis and Jessica caught him on the run a couple of times, too. But when he walked into Bill and Joy's house early one Saturday morning I'd just about had it. We tried everything. Talking, time-outs, stern "no-no's," swift swats on the fanny. Nothing worked.

Ultimately we decided imprisonment was the only answer.

I went to the hardware store and bought safety latches for every door in the house. We secured a door handle cover on the inside of his bedroom door to stop the nighttime roaming and put latches on every other door in the house. Yes, the pantry got latches, too.

Much to our delight Nathan got the idea. In fact, he got it so well he started using the same tactics on *us*. There are three doors in our home with locks on them: our bedroom door, the hall bathroom, and the downstairs door. They say children learn most through modeling, and that little guy modeled us without flaw. Every time we made a trip to our bedroom, hall bath, or downstairs we found the doors locked from the other side. Who says a three-year-old can't put two and two together? Since we had lost the keys to those doors years ago, we all became proficient at picking the locks with a screwdriver. If you happen to visit our home, you'll see a screwdriver permanently attached to the molding over our bedroom door. If you can't beat 'em, join 'em.

One frosty morning in November I was helping Jessie and Ben get ready for school when I glanced out the window to see little Nathan walking up the side lawn in bare feet. He was crying, confused, and didn't know what to do. Jessie had forgotten to latch the door after feeding the animals. There was our little wanderer, in his red pajamas, standing in the frozen grass with nothing to protect him from the cold.

I ran outside, brought him back to the house, bundled him in a blanket, and tried to calm him while he thawed out. His desperation brought tears to my eyes, because I knew he just didn't understand. He'd wanted to go outside to visit with the cat. He didn't know that he shouldn't leave the house without shoes and a coat in November. He didn't know it was only thirty degrees. He didn't know the white stuff on the grass would burn little bare feet. He just didn't know.

Now you and I may not waltz shoeless out of the house in November, or stroll uninvited into the neighbor's den, but we have other, more "sophisticated" ways of wandering. Sometimes, as with Nathan, we just don't know any better, and life teaches us not to try that shenanigan again. At other times we wander out of choice. We push the limits on purpose, thinking God's directions and boundaries are too strict, too rigid, too severe. We think they keep us from our freedom. I hear it over and over in the counseling office.

> *"It started out as just a simple one-night stand…"*
> *"I know lots of people who play with the numbers in their books…"*
> *"At the time, it seemed like the best way to handle the pregnancy…"*
> *"It was just a small lie…"*
> *"I had to try it, just once…"*
> *"It's vogue to read your horoscope…"*
> *"I only hit her because…"*

When we wander from our heavenly confines, we forget a fundamental truth. God gives us boundaries to keep the good in and the bad out. Those safety latches are for our protection. He knows when we wander from His ways that we end up confused and disoriented. We suffer. We lose quality of life. Relationships fly apart. We end up scared and broken. Part of our soul dies.

And Father God looks on, wanting so much more for us.

God knows better than anyone what it's like to have kids who wander. Moses said, "For the LORD your God…has known your wanderings" (Deuteronomy 2:7, NASB). He knows what it's like to hear his children cry out in the dark when they don't know where they are or how they got there.

He knows about the times we bolt for a new measure of freedom and wind up getting iced or burned.

He knows when we find ourselves standing in the middle of a situation—vulnerable, bare, and unprotected from the elements at large.

His eyes fill with tears, too.

When young David was on the run from jealous King Saul, he was forced to spend long months and *years* in hiding. Always on the run from place to place, he haunted the lonely wilderness like a lost soul, sometimes taking refuge in the depths of a limestone cave. And when the fear and anger intensified, his eyes turned toward Heaven. Eyes flowed with tears from a heart filled with grief. And with sore knees on the hard damp rocks of a cavern floor, he reminded himself of the truth:

> You've kept track of my every toss and turn through the sleepless nights, each tear entered in your ledger, each ache written in your book. (Psalm 56:8, The Message)

David says each tear is taken into account. In the Hebrew language the word used here reflects a picture of a vineyard keeper carefully watching for each drop squeezed from grapes by a wine press, as he creates a very costly wine. What that says to me is that God doesn't take our pain lightly. He isn't casual about our weeping. He isn't nonchalant about our suffering.

Each teardrop holds tremendous value.

When John and I were in Cairo, Egypt, we learned about various artifacts found in the Egyptian tombs. One item was called a lachrymatory, or "tear bottle." The custom in those ancient times was for friends to take tear bottles with them when they visited those who were ill or in great distress. As tears ran down the cheeks of the sufferer, friends caught the tears in the bottle and then sealed and preserved them as a memorial of the event.

I found that curious. There's a part of me that would prefer to *forget* the painful times of life. I'd rather give the joys more prominence in my mind than the sorrows. But David says God sees things differently. What I'd like to forget, God takes great care to remember.

What gave David the ability to endure years of oppression and hardship? A simple truth: *God remembers*. He keeps track. He remembers every sleepless night. He remembers every prayer, every groan, and every heartache too deep for words.

God remembers. That single thought changed David's fear-ridden, trembling words into a brand-new, confidant declaration. Following that pivotal thought David says:

Fearless now, I trust in God…. God, you did everything you promised, and I'm thanking you with all my heart. You pulled me from the brink of death, my feet from the cliff-edge of doom. Now I stroll at leisure with God in the sunlit fields of life. (vv. 11–13, The Message)

God isn't partial. What He did for David, He does for you and me. He remembers. When no one else knows we are suffering,

God does. He is with us, sitting by our side, catching the tears that roll off our cheeks. No sorrow goes undetected. In God's economy all suffering can serve an eternal purpose. Tears are *never* wasted. They are very carefully collected, sealed, and saved as a memorial by our Father in Heaven.

God also knows when you walk out of His house on a mission of your own. He is the One who assigns the neighborhood grandma to pray for you and the friend across the way to escort you home. He's the One who waves at the window for you to come back inside to get out of the cold. He's the One who longs for you to learn that His safety latches are there to keep the good in and the bad out.

An old hymn writer penned the words:

Prone to wander, Lord I feel it,
Prone to leave the God I love…

Maybe that's why Jesus made it so clear in His parable of the lost son in Luke 15:11–32.

Our God is a Father who welcomes wanderers home.

CHAPTER ELEVEN

THE SUNDAY MORNING BRIGADE

*Each of us should please his neighbor for his good,
to build him up.*
ROMANS 15:2

From the time we first met, John and I have been singing together.

It's always been something we've shared, something we've loved. We sang with the teenagers when John was a youth pastor. We sang in a traveling trio in college. We sang in the car to and from—wherever. During most of our married life we sang in front of the congregation as worship leaders.

But after Nathan was born, all that changed.

Frankly, I was just too depressed. Worship is a matter of the heart, and every time I set foot in the sanctuary and heard the music, I cried. I don't care who you are, it's embarrassing when you're on a platform where 5,000 people can watch you blubber. There is no polite way to wipe a runny nose without everyone noticing. The stage lights are so bright they reflect off even the smallest dribble. One time I tucked a hanky in my sleeve, just in case, and sure enough it was sopped halfway through worship.

But that wasn't the bad part.

Somehow it slipped out of my fingers and landed on the carpet in front of me...just out of comfortable reach. I wish you could have seen what happened from my vantage point.

Several hundred heads dropped in unison as they followed it to the ground. John was in the middle of a serious part in the service. It was all I could do to contain the giggles.

Finally I decided I needed a break. Actually I think the congregation needed a break from my emoting, so I stepped out of ministry for a while. It was for the best. Soon after, Nathan developed chronic ear and lung infections which made it impossible for me even to take him to church.

It wasn't long, however, before some kind ladies in the church figured out I was absent and called with an idea. Marylee said, "Pam, let's form a Sunday Morning Brigade. Give me the names of several ladies you'd like to come to your home to take care of Nathan so you can go to church. We'll each take one Sunday a month."

And that's just what happened. For the next year and a half, Marylee, Kathy, Margaret, and Joy came one Sunday a month to be with Nathan while I attended services. Sugar and Lynn stepped in to help, too. I can't tell you how much that two hours a week meant to me. They were hours I spent sitting in the congregation, crying through worship as the pain was purged from my soul. They were hours I soaked in Pastor Ted's words of strength, comfort, and hope. They were hours I leaned on the Holy Spirit to wrap words around my feelings and help me communicate with my Father.

Through that year God displayed His glory in a number of ways. It shined clearly each time one of the faithful four from the Sunday Morning Brigade showed up on my doorstep. It radiated when they held Nathan in their arms and lovingly spoke to him. It lit up the room every time I walked in from church with bloodshot eyes and they put their arms around me. I felt it in their compassion when they hugged me good-bye.

I think of Paul's words: "And we, who with unveiled faces all reflect the Lord's glory, are being transformed into his likeness with ever-increasing glory, which comes from the Lord, who is the Spirit" (2 Corinthians 3:18).

God reveals His glory in places and people. It shines into our life in a variety of ways. But whatever form it takes, it always makes a lasting impression, like a pattern burned into wood...an eternal impression of the One who will one day call us home to a glory that will never fade.

By the way, when we're all Over There, remind me to introduce you to the Sunday Morning Brigade. We'll all be enjoying worship together for a change...with no tears at all.

And Nathan Vredevelt may very well be leading the choir.

CHAPTER TWELVE

Taking Inventory

Are not two sparrows sold for a penny?
Yet not one of them will fall to the ground apart
from the will of your Father. And even the very hairs
of your head are all numbered. So don't be afraid.
MATTHEW 10:29–31

Certain things in life are predictable.

You can count on them happening at certain times and in certain ways. The sun rises, the sun sets. Rivers flow into the sea, owls hunt at night, bread falls butter-side down, and rain pours on the Portland Rose Parade.

And in the Vredevelt household, something else happens like proverbial clockwork...the way Nathan Vredevelt begins and ends his day.

When I hear Nathan stirring in the morning, I open his bedroom door and usually find him sitting in the rocker, looking at books or playing with a toy. His face lights up when I peek in, and after our hugs he routinely looks at me, shrugs his little shoulders, and says...

"Dada?"

I tell him his daddy is in the kitchen, or the shower, or wherever he happens to be at the moment.

"Bbbbbbb?"

That's his word for brother Ben, and I tell him what Ben is doing.

"Nana?"

That's what he calls his sister, Jessie, and before he does anything else, he wants an accounting of her whereabouts, too. For some reason it is very important for him to take inventory of his family as he starts his day.

Bedtime is like that, too. When it's time for him to crawl in for the night, he insists on giving *everyone* big hugs and kisses. Visitors, too. The few times I've tried to shuffle him off to bed prior to making these rounds you'd think I had committed a cardinal sin. He threw fits, frantically pointing to his mouth while demanding to see Dada, Bbbbb, and Nana. There was no chance for peace until he planted those kisses.

Nathan seems very tuned in to his family. When I rock him to sleep, in between songs I say, "Nathan, Mama loooooooooooooves you."

And without skipping a beat, he says, "Dada?"

"Yes, Nathan. Dada looooves you."

"Bbbbbb?"

"And Ben loooooves you."

"Nana?"

"And Jessie loooves you, too."

He likes this exchange so much that in the last couple of months he's begun adding others to the list. Now there's "Pa-pa" and "Em," our parents whom Jessie and Ben call Grandpa and Grandma, "Nnn" and "O," which are the boys' friends Andrew and Christopher, "Thhhh," otherwise known as Kelli buddy, who is like a big sister to all three of the kids, and "Mmmmm," short for Margaret, who has been his friend and helper on the days I work since he was five months old.

Morning and evening awaken a need in Nathan to take inventory of those who are most important to him, and he takes it very, very seriously.

Strange as it seems, an unpredictable turn of events can have the same effect on me.

Nathan's untimely arrival and diagnosis caused me to take inventory. I found myself standing at a crossroads, reconsidering my priorities and direction in life. I found myself asking, "What's most important?"

For the previous seven years I had served as the director of a Christian counseling center and counseled patients two days a week. I took a four-month leave of absence after Nathan's birth to adjust to being a family of five. Two weeks after returning to the counseling center I realized I no longer had the time, energy, or desire to serve as director, a job I had enjoyed over the years. I turned in my resignation shortly thereafter, knowing the job no longer fit me...and somewhat saddened by that fact. Even though it was part-time work, those hours and that energy needed to be invested at home.

My priorities changed, and so did my personal ambitions. I cared less about pleasing others and more about pleasing God and being true to myself and my family. I also cared less about accomplishments or position. I had written a book, which the publisher released at the same time Nathan was born. I remember the day my first copy arrived. I opened the package, flipped through the pages for a few seconds, and set it aside on the coffee table thinking, "That's nice."

A friend stopped by that afternoon to visit, saw it, and said, "Oh, *Pam!* Your new book is out! How exciting!" Tears filled my eyes, and all I could say was, "It means very little to me next to Nathan's life hanging in the balance."

During the year following Nathan's birth, I spent many hours reviewing and evaluating my involvements. I asked difficult questions: What were my motivations? Why was I involved in this, that, and the other? How was I doing as a wife and mother?

In short, I took a long hard look at *me*.

Some of the information that emerged from my reflections was encouraging. I could see how I'd grown and changed from a few years before. Other insights troubled me. I recognized an ugly pride in my soul and the need for humility. I saw the energy I spent trying to orchestrate and control and realized my need to let go and let God be God—and allow others their right to journey with less of my influence. I also realized I needed to yield my dreams and goals to God and give Him control of my agenda. That year of evaluation proved liberating for me; I felt I'd grown to another level.

But not without struggle.

I found the growth process to be a series of advances and retreats. Some days I moved forward at a pretty good clip. Other days I dug in my heels and threw a first-class tantrum. My greatest enemy in the process was my own selfishness. I didn't *want* to be inconvenienced. I didn't *want* to give up my sleep, energy, time, and interests. I didn't *want* Nathan to be handicapped. I didn't *want* to spend hours every week with three different therapists. I wanted Nathan to be N-O-R-M-A-L. I wanted the easier path I had been on before. "I...I...I...I..."

It wasn't much help to realize I'd seen this same preoccupation with self in other post-trauma victims in my counseling office. It happened time and again: A desire to shift their focus outward was turned back by the insistence and power of their pain.

—I saw the struggle in Sam, when he was diagnosed with terminal cancer.

—I saw it in Bonnie, when she was disabled after a car accident.

—I've seen it in scores of men and women after divorce... or during periods of chronic unemployment...or following the loss of a child. Like them, I found myself weary of the self-absorption. It was as though I was trying to push every button on the remote control unit, but the channel wouldn't change. The same painful images kept coming up on the screen. Images of what used to be. Images of the ideal rather than the real. Images of what I wanted for myself.

Anyone who has suffered loss from an unpredictable turn of events is going to struggle with introspection and self-absorption, at least for a season. It's built into the grief process. Devastating losses rivet our attention to our pain, just as a thumb screams for attention when smacked by a hammer. Even though I knew very well that this was part of the recovery process, I wanted so much to get on the other side of "myself" as fast as possible. I knew I would find freedom and rest easier there.

During that time I came across the records of a man who, like me, struggled with selfishness. His name was Paul. And he spoke candidly of the "mind wars" to the Christians in Galatia:

> My counsel is this: Live freely, animated and motivated by God's Spirit. Then you won't feed the compulsions of selfishness. For there is a root of sinful self-interest in us that is at odds with a free spirit, just as the free spirit is incompatible with selfishness. These two ways of life are antithetical, so that you cannot live at times one way and at times another way according to how you feel on any given day. Why don't you chose to be led by the Spirit and so escape the erratic compulsions?...
>
> What happens when we live God's way? He brings gifts into our lives, much the same way that fruit appears in an orchard—things like affection for others, exuberance about life, serenity. We develop a willingness to stick with things, a sense of compassion in the heart,

and a conviction that a basic holiness permeates things and people. We find ourselves involved in loyal commitments, not needing to force our way in life, able to marshal and direct our energies wisely. (Galatians 5:16–17, 22–23, The Message)

The choices Paul highlighted challenged me. I reasoned with myself: *If I surrender to my own selfish inclinations, I'll self-destruct. I'll stay stuck in this rut of introspection and lose freedom and forward movement. But if I choose to be led by the Spirit, I'll receive gifts from God which will shape and hone me to be more like Him.*

The answer seemed simple and obvious enough. But it's like they all say, easier said than done, because our selfishness and sense of justice keep getting in the way. When tragedies happen, we don't want to yield because there is a sense that we're somehow "giving in" to something unfair. It smacks against our sense of right and wrong. Obsessions are fueled as the mind works overtime to try to "fix" something that simply cannot be fixed, or to understand the "why's" which can never be fully understood this side of Heaven.

If we are to move beyond our preoccupation with self, there must be a time when we choose to yield. For me that meant saying, "I don't *like* where I am at this time in my life, but God, I choose to believe that You are leading me. I want to keep in step with You, so please show me how! Imprint Your image on my life today in whatever way You see fit."

Jesus said it more succinctly: "Not My will, but Yours be done."

When we yield to the Spirit of God, we can count on some eternal guarantees. He will quiet the mind wars. He will bring a healing so deep and so thorough that we will know it is His doing, and not ours. We'll hear the footsteps of that armed sentry pacing back and forth, standing perpetual guard duty outside the chambers of our soul—the very peace of Christ (Philippians 4:7). Our pain will take a backseat to God's purposes.

It's important to know that a better quality of life lies ahead, especially on days when we dread waking up in the morning and grief seems all-consuming. No matter how we feel about it on any given day (or night!), Paul assures us that we *will* see growth in our lives.

That's what taking inventory of our lives is all about. As believers in Jesus Christ, we're not to be like those who see only their circumstances and reckon their future on the shifting sand of life's vague probabilities. No, we're to build our very lives on the promises of God.

If you're not figuring *Him* into your life equation, the answer will always come out wrong.

CHAPTER THIRTEEN

"SOMEONE'S TALKING TO ME"

He is the source of every mercy
and the God who comforts us.
He comforts us in all our troubles
so that we can comfort others.
2 CORINTHIANS 1:3–4, NLT

My friend Dr. Ron Mehl relates an incident about Diane, a young woman with Down syndrome, the daughter of a man in his church.

> Dave Culver's daughter, Diane, lives in a group home in Salem, Oregon. Diane's mother was very ill, dying of cancer, and the situation was not improving. Dave decided to bring Diane home to Portland so she could visit her mom. After a short visit, Diane went back to Salem, but was very disturbed and emotional about the state of her mother's condition.
>
> Upon arriving at the group home, Diane asked if she could meet with Mary, a professional counselor for disabled people. Mary immediately noticed that Diane seemed troubled.
>
> "What's wrong, Diane?"
>
> "It's my mom," she answered. "I'm afraid my mother's going to die."
>
> As Diane proceeded to talk to the therapist about her

mom, she suddenly stopped, looked off into the distance, and a peaceful, serene look spread across her face.

"What is it, Diane?"

"Quiet!" she said, holding up her hand. "Someone's talking to me."

For a minute or so, not a word was spoken, and then the counselor finally asked, "Who is talking to you?"

"It was Jesus," Diane answered.

"What did He say?"

"He told me that He was going to take care of my mother and that everything would be all right."

From that moment on, Diane's demeanor changed. Her emotions were completely under control.

Some time later, Diane came back to Portland and was with the family when her mom, Anne, passed away. The night of the funeral, the house was filled with people. There were people sleeping everywhere, so they put a cot in her dad's room and she slept there.

About 2:30 in the morning Diane woke up, rose from the bed, and opened the door to the bedroom. Dave woke just in time to see her coming back into the room. He gently asked her what was wrong.

"I saw a bright light," Diane replied. "I thought someone left the TV on or something in the other room."

Dave was puzzled. Everyone was asleep; there was no TV, no light on anywhere in the house.

"What light?" Dave asked.

She looked at her dad and said, "It was Jesus. He told me that Mom's with Him now, and that she's just fine. He said she was His to take care of."

With that, Diane went back to bed and quickly fell asleep.

People often fabricate stories, create incredible plots, just for publicity and attention. But the young woman had no motive to create such a fantasy. Even her counselors, who are not Christians, said there was no way for her to stage a scene like that.[1]

When I first heard this story, I found myself slightly envious of the professional counselor who was with Diane when Jesus spoke to her. I wished I had been the one who witnessed her visitation! Nothing that dramatic has ever happened to one of *my* clients during a therapy hour.

But then again, I'm not sure how I would handle a situation like that. Would I laugh for joy, or weep in wonder? Would I sit calmly and objectively nod my head like a well-trained professional, or leave my chair and hug my sister in Christ to whom God revealed His glory? Knowing me, I'd likely do all the above.

I'm not sure who got paid for services at the therapist's office that day...but I know Who deserves the credit.

His name is Wonderful Counselor.

CHAPTER FOURTEEN

NO TURNING BACK

When you go through deep waters and great trouble,
I will be with you.
ISAIAH 43:2, NLT

For a season, I longed for the path I was on before.

But there was no going back.

Nathan's arrival set in motion a whole new set of circumstances that would shape us all for the rest of our lives. There was no use wishing things were different. His Down syndrome was an undeniable reality of life.

I recall several times when Jessie and Ben said, "I wish Nathan didn't have Down syndrome." One evening Ben prayed, "God please take Nathan's Down syndrome away." A week after Nathan was born, I took Jessie out to breakfast and explained what the doctors had told us about Down syndrome and mental retardation.

She thought for a minute and with fearful eyes said, "Mom, are the kids at school going to make fun of him?"

I told her Nathan likely would be teased, just as she and Ben had been teased, but we would help him learn how to handle it, just as we had helped them. (I hoped in my heart that that would be possible.) And I reminded Jessie—and myself—that when Nathan had hard days, God would be there for him, too.

I found comfort reading stories which underlined the

promise of God's presence. I reviewed the story of Moses, particularly the time when he didn't want to return to the land of the Pharaohs for fear of what might happen to him. He knew his enemies were waiting for a chance to plant him six feet under the Egyptian sand—without a pyramid on top! That's when God said to Moses, "I will certainly be with you" (Exodus 3:12, NKJV).

I reflected on the story of Joshua, when he assumed the leadership of Israel after Moses died. He had lost his mentor and intimate friend. There was no one closer to Moses. It was Joshua whom Moses asked to accompany him to Mt. Sinai when it was time to receive the Ten Commandments. Moses had helped shape Joshua from a youngster rough around the edges into a man full of faith, courage, vision, and the Spirit of God. Joshua had barely finished saying good-bye to Moses when God commissioned him. What insecurity and apprehension he must have felt as he set his face toward the horizon of the promised land and heard God say, "Lead on."

But God knew the anxiety in his heart and quieted his struggle with these words: "As I was with Moses, so I will be with you. I will not leave you nor forsake you" (Joshua 1:5, NKJV).

I remembered some verses I memorized in Bible college where God made a promise to the children of Israel as they were enduring years of chronic suffering:

> Now, this is what the LORD says—
>   he who created you...
>   he who formed you...
> "Fear not, for I have redeemed you;
>   I have summoned you by name; you are mine.
> When you pass through the waters,
>   I will be with you;

and when you pass through the rivers,
>   they will not sweep over you.
When you walk through the fire,
>   you will not be burned;
>   the flames will not set you ablaze.
For I am the LORD, your God,
>   the Holy One of Israel, your Savior....
Do not be afraid, for I am with you."

>   (Isaiah 43:1–3, 5)

I couldn't tell Jessie that morning in the restaurant that Nathan would never be mistreated. I knew otherwise. But I *could* tell her that God would be with him, and He would be with all of us as Nathan grew up in our family. That seemed to help.

Three years later Jessie and her teacher invited me to talk to her fourth grade class about Down syndrome. She wanted the children to meet Nathan. When we arrived, he quickly spotted Jessie and crawled up on her lap.

Moving to the front of the room, I asked the group: "How many of you have ever been called a 'retard'?"

All of them raised their hands. We defined the word "retard" to mean slow, not stupid. They learned that some children are born with physical problems that make them grow and develop more slowly than others, but that they are just as important and valuable as anyone else. They heard that each of them was special because God made them and He had a very important purpose for each of their lives. It didn't matter if they learned fast or slow, were athletic or musical, loved or hated math, or thought they were good-looking or ugly. God loved them all just the same.

One little boy raised his hand and asked, "But *why* was

Nathan born with Down syndrome?"

He was bold enough to ask what the rest of us wondered in secret. I told him I didn't understand all the "why's," but I did find one reason in John, chapter nine. I opened my Bible and read verses 1 through 3 to them:

> As he went along, he saw a man blind from birth. His disciples asked him, "Rabbi, who sinned, this man or his parents, that he was born blind?"
>
> "Neither this man nor his parents sinned," said Jesus, "but this happened so that the work of God might be displayed in his life."

I told them I believed God had a special purpose for Nathan's life and that somehow He would use his Down syndrome to accomplish His purpose. I also told them I believed God had a special purpose for each of them being born, too, and He would use all their strengths—and even their weaknesses—for a good cause if they would let Him.

At the end of our time together Nathan walked up and down the aisles, slapping high-fives with each of the children. Ryan, the boy sitting next to Jessie, leaned over to her and said, "Jessie, you've got an awesome little brother!" That put a mile-wide smile on Jessie's face.

Come to think of it, it was the very same kind of smile I saw on Nathan's face when he saw the angel in our living room.

It must be a Heaven thing.

CHAPTER FIFTEEN

An Untimely Visitation

*An angel of the God to whom I belong
and whom I serve stood beside me.*
ACTS 27:23, NLT

It was one of those dark, February mornings where the sky sags under its own weight down to the level of Oregon rooftops.

It was Sunday, but we didn't go to church because John and Nathan had the flu. *Everyone* was grumpy, and as the morning passed, things went from bad to worse.

Benjamin was playing Nintendo and had finally conquered a level he'd been trying to master for weeks. He was elated. But he turned ballistic a few seconds later when Nathan chose to push the restart button...which in one merciless second wiped out everything his big brother had accomplished in a morning of skillful labors.

Benjamin couldn't believe his eyes. When the reality finally hit home, he stormed up the stairs in a rage, yelling, "Moooooom! Nathan just wrecked my game!" I asked Ben to take a ten minute time-out on his bed to cool down while I disciplined Nathan.

I found the little offender by the Nintendo controls, guilt written all over his face.

He knew exactly what he had done, and he knew it was wrong. This had happened many times before. I gave him a good scolding and a ten minute time-out. While he sat on his stool waiting for the timer to buzz, I remembered I needed to talk with Jessie about completing some responsibilities before she left for a party at one o'clock. But instead of a simple, "Okay," she began reciting every reason known to humankind why she didn't want to do what was asked. (She was definitely hormonal.)

Nathan, in the meantime, was howling on his time-out stool. Ben was pitching a fit on his bed. Jessie went on playing "Let's Make a Deal" with me—which was every bit as annoying as a temper tantrum. And *I* was ready to submit my letter of resignation—to whomever.

Gathering and reknotting my composure about me like a rumpled bathrobe, I sat with Ben on his bed and tried to validate his frustrations. No, I soothed, being a big brother was certainly not an easy assignment. I told him how sorry I was Nathan had wrecked his game and that I understood why he felt angry. He said the just punishment for Nathan's crime should have been an *all day* time-out. I tried my best not to laugh and asked if he would play the game again so I could watch him beat the levels.

I also told him I'd help load the dishwasher, which was his job for the morning. He continued to vent as he none-too-gently plunked the plates into the racks. As we continued our rather loud discussion amongst the clatter of dishes, Nathan bolted into the room with shining eyes.

"Mama! *Mama!*" he said with urgency and excitement.

When I looked over at him, he tapped his shoulders with his hands and made a flapping motion out to the side, like children do who are pretending to fly. That's sign language for "angel."

"Nathan," I said slowly, "do you see an angel?"

He nodded vigorously and pointed past me and Benjamin, through the doorway between the kitchen and the living room.

His eyes were fixed on something, and he wanted Ben and me to see, too.

"Do you see an angel in the living room?"

A sparkly smile lit his face, and he shook his head up and down.

"Well, Nathan," I sighed, "we could certainly *use* an angel or two in this house today."

It had been more than eight months since the last time Nathan had told us he had seen an angel. We hadn't been talking about angels that morning, and please understand that Nathan simply does not possess the cognitive skills to fabricate reality. In another child you might suspect that type of announcement as a ruse to draw attention from bad behavior. But that sort of deception is beyond Nathan. If he initiates conversation about something, it is always something concrete that he can *see*. Abstract concepts are not a part of his experience.

I had often wondered if the angel sightings would end as he grew older, and I was encouraged to know that Nathan was still graced with this perception. On the whole, it didn't seem like a big deal to him. Just your average, run-of-the-mill occurrence. About as extraordinary as the arrival of the UPS guy at the front door. Perhaps Nathan had witnessed more in the spirit realm than he had told us and this instance was "nothing unusual."

But for me, the *timing* of this particular angel (or angels!) was very significant.

We were all grumpy and out of sorts. Butting heads, raising our voices. We had skipped church. Some of us were sick. And I was about as discouraged as I had been in a long time. Frankly, our home didn't seem a very likely place for an angelic visitation. It was easier for me to picture an angel dropping in on Billy Graham's family or peeking in on the church service we had just missed. Surely the angel would rather be some-where more "godly" than the Vredevelts' battlefield.

I've always understood that angels are God's messengers, sent to minister to His children. Even the word *angel* means "messenger." I'm not sure exactly what message I was supposed to receive that day, but one thing was very clear to me. God wanted us to know that He was with us—

in the midst of the chaos…
in the midst of our imperfections…
in the midst of our angry words…
in the midst of our jangled nerves…
in the midst of my pity party.

On a dark winter morning, on a day that seemed anything but divine, in an atmosphere that seemed anything but heavenly, Heaven dispatched a representative. And the only one who had eyes to see was a little observer with Down syndrome named Nathan.

The "untimely" appearance reminded me of something the apostle Paul had experienced in the first-century city of Corinth. He was on assignment for God when he suddenly found himself tangling with the very people he so passionately longed to serve.

Paul had devoted himself to preaching and testifying to the Jews that Jesus was the Christ. He was doing just what God had told him to do. But he wasn't well received. There was no acceptance. No appreciation. No applause. No kindness. Just resistance and opposition. Actually, Paul called it abuse:

But when the Jews opposed Paul and became abusive, he shook out his clothes in protest and said to them, "Your blood be on your own heads! I am clear of my

responsibility. From now on I will go to the Gentiles."
(Acts 18:6)

It looks to me as though Paul had "had enough" of the
Corinthian Jews. His words ring with anger and resignation.
Somehow I don't think he expected that kind of a response to
his sacrificial service. Abuse? He'd been pouring out his time,
energy, and resources for their good! He was seeking nothing
but their eternal salvation.

Had we caught up with him that day outside the syna-
gogue, I think we might have seen a man kicking sand, dis-
gusted with life, apprehensive about the future, and wishing
mightily for a different assignment. From the looks of things he
was ready to quit. He didn't want to push the restart button on
the game; he wanted to rip the plug right out of the wall. That's
when the Lord spoke to Paul in a vision:

> "Do not be afraid; keep on speaking, do not be silent.
> For I am with you, and no one is going to attack and
> harm you." (Acts 18:9–10)

From that point forward, Paul was a different man. He was
energized by the conviction that God was with him. He tapped
into a source of boundless determination. He had the *oomph* to
keep putting one foot in front of the other on his God-given
path. In spite of abusive attacks. In spite of the mudslinging
majority. In spite of power struggles, exhaustion, and discouragement. In spite of seeing very few results from his efforts.
The man found a fresh supply of *staying power.*

After Paul heard from God that night we read: "So Paul
stayed for a year and a half, teaching them the word of God"
(Acts 18:11).

That's what happens when we remember that God is with us. We have staying power. Meaning. Purpose and direction. The awareness of God's presence gives us strength to face whatever lies ahead. We experience a rekindling of the desire and ability to continue on the course we've been assigned. Resignation letters line the bottom of the trash can, where they belong.

None of us know what the future holds. Unforeseen events lie dark and shapeless on our horizon. The road may very well get rough before it gets smooth. Here in the Vredevelt household, we can't predict when or if Nathan will see another angel. I do hope the next visitation will find us in a less chaotic state than the last one.

But then again, though angels may come and go on missions beyond our understanding, the Lord Jesus said, "I am with you *always*." That ought to provide all the staying power you and I will ever need.

Even on a blue Sunday.

CHAPTER SIXTEEN

THAT FARAWAY LOOK

I pray also that the eyes of your heart
may be enlightened.
EPHESIANS 1:18

If you've ever spent time around people with Down syndrome, you know that every now and then they turn their faces toward Heaven and get a faraway look in their eyes. Sometimes it appears they're carrying on a conversation, even though no one else is in the room.

Each time this has happened with Nathan, I've felt a quiet sense of wonder. What was he saying? To whom was he speaking? Just what was transpiring? Was there a heavenly visitor in the room I couldn't see? Did a guardian angel prompt the spontaneous smiles that crossed his face? Was a window in the heavens open to him? What was being discussed in those lengthy conversations with "the air"?

As Nathan nears kindergarten age, he is better able to ask for what he needs and wants. Sometimes with sketchy words, but mostly with sign language. Whenever we sit down at the table for a meal, Nathan clasps his hands and shakes them in the air, which is his way of reminding us we need to pray and give thanks for our food. Whenever he takes a tumble and hurts himself, he runs to John or me, clasps his hands, and asks us to pray for him.

Not long ago one of the neighbor boys, Christopher, was

playing at our home and scraped his knee on the cement. We brought him inside, cleaned up the bloody mess, and applied a Band-Aid to the injury. Nathan stood by with wide eyes, watching the operation intently. That night when I put him to bed, he clasped his hands together in front of my face.

"O," he said, which means Christopher.

We prayed together that the Lord would heal Christopher's sore knee and help him feel better.

Before Nathan was born, we discussed various names for him and finally decided on Nathan Charles Vredevelt. Nathan means "gift of God." Charles means "spiritual perception." In spite of the many hardships, we all agree that Nathan is a gift given to our family by the Lord. His weaknesses have driven us to a deeper dependency on God. This assignment is beyond our natural resources. His spiritual perception has challenged our faith and sensitized us to the spiritual realm in new and fresh ways.

My friend Mari Hanes knew this would happen when she saw Nathan as a newborn. Mari is a discerning pastor's wife, author, and prayer warrior. We talked together one afternoon as I was deep in grief over Nathan's diagnosis. She saw Nathan in my arms and said, "Pam, I sense the Spirit of the Lord all over this baby. There will be many wonders ahead for you...."

I didn't fully understand the meaning of her words, but they brought comfort. Now, nearly five years later, I am beginning to understand. I say *beginning*, because I think we have yet to see what God's plans and purposes are for this little boy.

It all makes me wonder...

I wonder about the future. I wonder about the present. I wonder what Nathan sees when he gives me the sign for "angel." I wonder what he is thinking when his eyes seem to focus on something out of my range of perception. I wonder if he might be praying something like this...

Lord, Mom and Dad are still having a few doubts about my heavenly friends—but they're making progress! I like it when Your angels visit. They remind me of my real home—the Home You've told me about—and make me happy. Mommy told me that she and Dad wish they could see angels, too. But I don't think that's a good idea. Their faith grows more by NOT seeing them. So Lord, let's just keep the angels between You and me. I like watching Mommy and Daddy grow.

When he looks out the window for miles on end as we drive to therapy each week, I wonder if he's thinking something like…

Lord, I like my special teachers. They believe in me. They tell me, "Nathan, you can do it!" When I see their confidence in me, it makes me want to try hard. Thank You for Margaret. When she helps Mom take me to therapy, she studies everything they do so she can tell Mommy. Bless Margaret, dear Lord, like she blesses me. Save some extra special crowns with big shiny jewels just for her. I think she is going to need a wheelbarrow when she gets to Heaven. Her two hands won't be enough to carry all the rewards You'll have for her.

I wonder what he's thinking at Jessie's and Ben's basketball games. If he could form his words, would he be saying something like this?

Lord, I want to play, too. I know I'm not as fast, and I don't catch the ball well. But I love to play. Why are people so concerned about winning? Aren't games supposed to be fun? I don't understand why people get angry and yell at the children and referees. I feel sad for them. They've lost their joy and forgotten what is more important. Maybe when I get older You'll let me play on a team. I'll remind them that people are more important than points.

At night in the rocking chair as I sing him to sleep, I wonder if he tells the Lord something like…

Thank You for giving me this mission on earth. Thank You for helping Mommy and Daddy when they don't know what to do. Thank You for helping them when they are tired, sad, and afraid. You are changing them. They are softer, more kind and understanding. My weaknesses are making them more like You.

But a mission this big can make me tired, too! Good night, Lord. We'll start fresh in the morning.

CHAPTER SEVENTEEN

WORDS IN A SAFE PLACE

He knows the secrets of every heart.
PSALM 44:21, NLT

Throw all your anxiety upon Him,
for His concern is about you.
1 PETER 5:7, MLB

It must be hard not to be able to speak. I can sense Nathan's frustration as he struggles to maneuver his mouth to tell me what is very clear in his mind.

Today his conflict went beyond frustration.

When John put a piece of toast in front of him, he started crying, banging his head with his hands, and groaning something we couldn't understand. We usually find a way to decode his messages, but this time we were stumped. As big tears streamed down his face, I sighed and said to John, "I wish Nathan could talk. So much of him is locked inside unable to get out."

Little Nathan, however, isn't alone in his frustration. And Down syndrome isn't the only malady that prevents people from speaking, or keeps wants and needs and hurts and lonely places bottled up inside. I think you'll understand more when you meet three other fellow travelers who learned the secret about secrets.

There was the little boy in Malawi...

John went with six other church members to this tiny African nation to help some missionaries establish a new fellowship. Each morning they canvassed the neighborhoods, inviting villagers to come to evening open-air crusades.

As the team made its way through one corner of a village, a crowd of nationals surrounded them. One of the team members noticed a seven-year-old boy who kept pushing his way through the crowd, trying to grab the Scripture booklets from people's hands. Since the team had limited supplies, the booklets were given only to the adults, who were to read them to the children.

But this little guy was persistent. No, he was downright *rude*, shoving and elbowing anyone who got in his way. When he finally reached the team, several of the national women pointed to the boy and said, "He has a demon. The boy hasn't spoken from birth."

The villagers weren't sharing that bit of information as "an interesting fact." With the interpreter's help, the team finally understood that the people expected them to *do* something for this little boy.

As the group gathered around him, one of the ladies knelt down and talked to him about Jesus. Then they laid hands on him and prayed that the demons would leave and that Jesus would come into his heart. After a big "Amen," that little boy hugged the Scripture book to his heart, looked up at all the people around him, and with tears in his eyes spoke his first words:

"Jesus loves me! Jesus loves me! Jesus loves me!"

Word got around, and that night all the villagers from that corner of town were at the crusade. By the end of the week over 1,300 Malawi grandmas, grandpas, moms, dads, and kids accepted Jesus as their Savior and Lord.

Can you imagine the earful that little boy's mom and dad got in the days that followed? Seven years worth of stockpiled stories! I doubt very much that they said, "Run along and play now. We'll talk about it later."

Things are different in America. People are locked up in other ways. I see it each week in the counseling office. Not in little boys who have speech impairments, but in people like you and me. I'm talking about typical, get-up-in-the-morning, go-to-work, raise-the-kids kinds of people. Moms who help with PTA. Dads who coach Little League. Brothers. Sisters. Aunts. Uncles. Normal folks on the outside, but locked up on the inside.

There was Kay…

…the forty-six-year-old woman who told me about Matthew, the baby she had lost fourteen years ago in stillbirth. Her family had said, "It's over. Forget it. *Don't talk about it.* We have to move on."

And that's exactly what she did. She moved on. Stayed busy. Got involved in things. Kept her mind occupied. Only…she didn't move on emotionally. Her heart was tightly wedged in an incident long past. She was frozen in time, arrested in grief. Matthew's name hadn't been mentioned since the day she left the hospital. Unlike the way little Faith Christina's arrival and departure were handled, this family wanted no funeral, no memorial, no pictures, no words spoken. The incident was treated *as if it had never happened.* Even the cards sent by friends had been ignored—and promptly burned. The family thought that erasing the evidence would erase the pain.

But it didn't. It couldn't.

So now there were fourteen years of stockpiled pain, locked up inside, unable to get out. No wonder she was having panic attacks! No wonder she felt she was about to burst. The human heart was never designed to deal with sorrow that way! For the first time in fourteen years, Kay found the courage to break the "no talk" family rule, crack open the door, and risk talking about Matthew.

As the secret was broken, so was the power of the pain.

There was Marissa...

...who was oh-so-good at keeping secrets. Not because she wanted to, but because it was how she'd learned to survive. She had been sexually abused by her father from the time she was a little girl, and she didn't dare tell her secret. If she did, her father said he would put her in jail and kill her mother. Little girls believe their big, strong daddies. In Marissa's innocent mind, there were no other options. She had to be a good little girl. And part of being so very good was "keeping the secret."

But that terrible secret, buried for so many years and land-scaped over the top with neat shrubbery and little flowers, became like a hidden toxic waste dump. The poison leeched into the very soil of her life, gradually numbing and warping her soul. Even the good parts. I saw evidence of the hidden toxins in words such as...

I want to enjoy my husband and kids, but—I have no feelings."
"It's like—I'm numb. Flat. I can't tell the difference between happy and sad."
"Nothing matters to me—even though I *want* it to matter."
I used to be passionate and sensitive. I used to care.
What's wrong with me? It's not like me not to care."

You see, we weren't built to bury our feelings alive! We weren't designed to live by a "no talk" rule. The mind has limitations built into its defense system. If we block the bad, we also block the good. The result?

No sorrow...but no joy either.
No heartache...but no passion for life as well.
No grief...but no capacity for laughter.
It all gets locked up together.

The good news is, we have a key to unlocking our pain, and it's right in our pocket. The key is telling our secrets to someone safe. A trusted friend, a pastor, and a therapist can help. *But there is no one safer than our Lord,* because He already knows the secrets of the heart (Psalm 44:21).

The writer of Hebrews reminds us that God's eyes miss *nothing:*

Nothing in all creation is hidden from God's sight.
Everything is uncovered and laid bare before the eyes of
him to whom we must give account. (Hebrews 4:13)

He sees. He knows. He feels. He understands our secrets better than anyone. And with that knowledge He encourages you and me to approach Him, to sit at His side, to disclose the burdens of our heart. Not sheepishly. Not with fear in our eyes and a catch in our throat. But with our head held high, confident that we will be welcomed and embraced.

Therefore, since we have a great high priest who has gone through the heavens, Jesus the Son of God, let us hold firmly to the faith we profess. For we do not have a high priest who is unable to sympathize with our weaknesses, but we have one who has been tempted in every way, just as we are—yet was without sin. Let us then approach the throne of grace with confidence, so that we may receive mercy and find grace to help us in our time of need. (Hebrews 4:14–16)

Have you ever thought about the writer's divinely inspired choice of words in that passage? *Sympathize...weaknesses... throne of grace...confidence...mercy...grace...need*

Consider also what the writer of Hebrews DIDN'T say. He didn't say "throne of hell, fire, and brimstone." He didn't say "throne of judgment." He didn't say "throne of wrath."

God chooses His words very carefully, and the words He chose were "throne of grace."

That means a place of kindness, blessing, and unmerited, unlimited favor. It's a *safe* place. It's a place where we can expect to find mercy and compassion. It's a place where God will delight to hear our secrets and meet our needs.

But there's a catch! We have to take the key out of our pocket and *use* it! We have to stick it in the throne room door, turn it, push the door open, and walk in. We can't stay outside and expect to get the goods. We have to risk. We have to approach Him. We have to take the first step.

James said it in different words: "Come near to God and he will come near to you" (James 4:8).

When I read through Psalms, it is clear to me that David knew the secret to unlocking the troubles in his heart, and he used the key every hour of the day. Listen...

As for me, I shall call upon God,
And the LORD will save me.

Evening and morning and at noon, I will complain and
murmur,
And He will hear my voice.
He will redeem my soul in peace from the battle which
is against me.
Cast your burden upon the LORD, and He will sustain
you.

(Psalm 55:16–18,22, NASB)

David said he called on God in the evening, morning, and
at noon. All day long he brought his complaints, his struggles,
his conflicts, and his pain to the One who sits on the throne of
grace. And even through the long hours of the night, he
poured out his heart to the One who hears. Not to friends. Not
to family. Not to therapists. But to the One who knew everything that transpired in his life.

Please don't misunderstand me. I do believe it is critical for
our emotional and spiritual health that we learn to share our
difficulties with safe people. But we have an even *bigger* need to
cultivate a safe place with God because there will be times
when others simply won't be available, won't understand,
won't really listen, or won't know what to do with what we tell
them.

God is always available. He always understands. He always
knows how to handle our secrets. He is never shocked or dis-
mayed by what we tell Him.

People can help, but only God can heal. His presence is the
safest place of all.

The little boy in Malawi found that safe place. So did a
couple of ladies named Kay and Marissa. The process started in
a therapist's office, but it ended up in the throne room. *That* is
where the pain lost its power.

John and I have been told by speech therapists that our Nathan may always struggle with speaking. Words may be a daunting challenge to him the rest of his life. That's one reason why we plan to teach him about that key in his pocket as early as possible. We want him to know there is One who always understands. When we can't decode his message, God's got the meaning down pat. Interpreters aren't necessary around the throne.

When we can't make sense of Nathan's groans, there is One who comprehends every detail of what is bothering him. And He will help Nathan even when he doesn't know what to say, when there is only a deep undercurrent of feeling that can't shape itself into words.

As Nathan learns to share the secrets of his heart with his Heavenly Father, we find strength in knowing that *God* will sustain him. It's not all up to us.

In truth, it never has been.

CHAPTER EIGHTEEN

ACCEPTING A
NEW DESTINATION

*I have learned to be content, whatever the circumstances may be.
I know now how to live when things are difficult and I know how
to live when things are prosperous. In general and in particular
I have learned the secret of...facing either plenty or poverty.
I am ready for anything through the strength of the
One who lives within me.*

PHILIPPIANS 4:11–13, PHILLIPS

When Nathan was born, cards and letters poured in from family
and friends. They wanted so much to help and share in our
grief. One letter enclosed a clipping from the newspaper that
challenged me to open my heart to the new direction my life
had taken. It helped me see that so much of my anguish was
caused by my own resistance.

Being in a tug of war with the events or circumstances in
our life does not change things. What is, IS. Trying to escape or
leave the present doesn't help either. But I know something
that *does* help.

Acceptance.

Acceptance doesn't make things harder; it makes them easier.
It empowers us to see with a new set of eyes. Emily Perl
Kingsley said it beautifully in a little story she penned years
ago.

She begins by saying that when you're going to have a

baby, it's like planning a fabulous vacation. Then as the wheels of the jumbo jet touch down, you awaken from your slumber and hear a cheery flight attendant saying, "Welcome to Holland."

"HOLLAND?!" you say. "What do you mean, *Holland?* I signed up for Italy! I'm supposed to be in Italy. All my life I've dreamed of going to Italy."

But there's been a change in the flight plan. They've landed in Holland and there you must stay.

The important thing is that they haven't taken you to a horrible, disgusting, filthy place, full of pestilence, famine, and disease. It's just a *different* place.

So you must go out and buy new guidebooks. And you must learn a whole new language. And you will meet a whole new group of people you would never have met.

It's just a different place. It's slower-paced than Italy, less flashy than Italy. But after you've been there awhile and catch your breath, you look around, and you begin to notice that Holland has windmills. Holland has tulips. Holland even has Rembrandts.

But everyone you know is busy coming and going from Italy, and they're all bragging about what a wonderful time they had there. And for the rest of your life, you will say, "Yes, that's where I was supposed to go. That's what I had planned."

And the pain of that will never, ever, ever go away, because the loss of that dream is a very significant loss. But if you spend your life mourning the fact that you didn't get to Italy, you may never be free to enjoy the special, and very lovely things about Holland.[1]

I had occasion to think about that "unintended Holland trip" when I found myself sitting at a preschool classroom table with my knees in my throat. Preschool chairs are not made for adult women five feet seven inches tall.

But it didn't matter. This was a special occasion; my youngest son Nathan had invited me to a Mother's Day tea.

It had been years since I attended my first celebration as a mom. I remember watching little Jessie with her pink polka-dot dress and blond ponytail sing the special music just for Mom. With total confidence she stood in the front row and belted out the songs at the top of her lungs. Watching her perform I thought, *She's so bubbly and full of life. None of this intimidates her.*

And then there was the time Ben played Joseph in the kindergarten Christmas program. He was given the assignment of pulling Mary, who was inside a cardboard donkey which she carried around her waist, several times around the stage. This was supposed to represent their long journey to Bethlehem.

The teacher had told them to park the donkey stage left before walking over to the manger, stage right. When Ben/Joseph tugged on the rope to park the donkey as per instructions, however, he hit a snag. Mary, with a mind of her own, assertively leaned back in her donkey, refusing to budge. But Joseph was a man on a mission and wasn't about to be bullied. So he hauled off and gave a turbo-charged yank on the rope, which propelled a startled Mary three feet forward. Infuriated, Mary threw down her donkey, slammed her hands on her hips, gave Joseph a *very* dirty look, and stomped off-stage.

So much for an angelic nativity scene. Ben/Joseph, stunned by Mary's unpredictable mood swing, stomped over to the manger and planted a huge pout on his face. And so goes the story of Mary and Joseph's first fight.

Many times I've watched Jessie and Ben on stage, and laughed and cried, soft touch that I am. Seeing them perform made me one proud mom. After the formal presentations they usually served me coffee and cookies and guided me around the classroom to see what they had made for the occasion. They were proud I had come and proud I was their mother.

This time around, I knew it would be different.

This time it would be Holland, not Italy.

I knew Nathan wouldn't be able to articulate the words of the songs and would probably miss some hand motions here and there. I knew the twenty extra mothers in the classroom would upset his predictable routine and shake his confidence. I wasn't at all sure how the morning would go...but I made an important decision before I ever walked through that class-room door.

I decided to open my heart to whatever was ahead and to accept it with gratitude.

Acceptance is powerful. It brings quiet peace to a heart torn with conflict. It comes when we make a simple choice to take a deep breath and say, "We are exactly where we are supposed to be at this moment in time." It means we stop wasting precious time and emotional energy wishing things were different, or longing to be someone else, or wanting another set of circum-stances. It's a force for change that can turn bad into good. It's the door to joy and contentment. It's trusting that "my times are in Your hand" (Psalm 31:15, NKJV).

The circumstance doesn't matter. It may be singleness. Or widowhood. Or a heartbreaking marriage. Or infertility. Or disa-bility. Or a lingering illness. Or *any* life situation in which we find ourselves and over which we have no control. With Paul we learn to say, "I have learned to be content whatever the circumstances" (Philippians 4:11).

And not just content. But truly thankful.

When the children presented their songs at teatime, Nathan stood at my side and made his best effort to say a few syllables. His hand motions weren't well defined, but they were consistent. His pudgy little hand gripped my shirt, and he smiled much of the time. He was enjoying this! During one of the songs I glanced at another mom who happened to be watching Nathan. She had sad tears in her eyes. I'm not sure what she was thinking, but a spontaneous insight bubbled to the surface as I witnessed this event.

Yes, I realized I was in a "different place," and not one of my choosing. That much was clear. But I also realized that *God* was in this different place, *and that He had brought me here.*

After the presentation I took Nathan by the hand and guided him around the room to view his artwork on the walls. I pointed to his pictures and said, "Very nice, Nathan!" And then he proceeded to bring me one cookie after another from the silver tray. Between the two of us, we must have eaten a dozen. The limit was two. Oh well.

I felt a deep sense of gratitude when I left the school that day. Gratitude to God for helping me move through years of grief toward more acceptance.

That doesn't mean I don't feel sad now and then. I do.

That doesn't mean I never play the "What if?" game. I do.

That doesn't mean I never daydream about "Italy." I do.

But less now. Less than before.

I am grateful that God has taught our family to perceive Nathan's differences as uniquenesses to be appreciated and understood. I am grateful that the joy over what Nathan can do far surpasses the sadness over what he cannot do. But most of all, I am grateful that God has given "the handicapped boy in the class" (as some refer to him) to me, and that he's proud I'm his mom.

There's a lot of love in Holland.

EXPECTATIONS

In the morning, O Lord, you hear my voice;
in the morning I lay my requests before you
and wait in expectation.

PSALM 5:3

They say you get what you expect. But then, what do "they" know, anyway?

—Launi expected to be married happily ever after. It didn't happen.

—Tammy, Jackie, Martin, and Len expected their partners to be faithful. They weren't.

—Bob and Dave expected their company revenues to increase 25 percent last year. They both filed for bankruptcy instead.

—Karen and Phil expected their son to go to college in the fall. He died in a motorcycle accident this spring.

—Dace, Mira, Judy, and I expected to give birth to healthy babies. Yet all of our children have special needs.

An Old Testament gentleman named Job had some expectations, too. And he also felt the bone-deep ache of disappointment when they didn't come about. At one point he penned in his journal: "When I expected good, then evil came; when I waited for light, then darkness came" (Job 30:26, NASB).

After Nathan was born, I took him to Dr. Eki for a checkup and found he needed immunization shots. The nurse explained the risks and ramifications and quoted some statistics. One out of every so many children (some astronomical number) have adverse reactions. This information, I knew, was supposed to comfort me and assure me that all would be fine. But my mind went another direction. We had *already* broken the odds by having a child with Down syndrome. Who was to say we wouldn't break the odds again?

Trauma tends to break down your defenses. It makes it hard to expect much of anything, for fear of being disappointed all over again. We went ahead with the shots…but not without anxiety.

The truth is…

—*I can't expect* Nathan to read a book out loud as Jessie and Ben did when they were in kindergarten. If I hang on to that expectation, I will be disappointed. But I CAN expect him to read. That is a tangible, reachable goal for him.

—*I can't expect* John and me to be empty nesters in ten to fifteen years, as we had previously thought. But I CAN expect that whatever comes will in some way be good and that God will be with us.

—*I can't expect* myself to do as much for John, Jessie, and Ben as I did before Nathan joined our family. Their needs have changed. And so have mine. I'm dividing my energies between four rather than three. But the whole is greater than the sum of the parts. Nathan has added more to the family than he has taken away. We all have made adjustments, and the experience we share is rich. Different than we expected, yes, but rich.

—*I can't expect* myself to always be a wise, patient, attentive mother and wife. That's what I want to be, but many times I fall short. When I'm tired, I snap at my kids. When they give me flack, I raise my voice. Even though I try very hard, I'm not always who or what I want to be.

That's about the time I realize once again how profound and desperate is my need for God and His power to change me. That's when I have to hold tightly to the expectation that the work He has started in me He will finish. That's when I must stand on the promise that His power in me "is able to carry out His purpose and do superabundantly, far over and above all that we dare ask or think—infinitely beyond our highest prayers, desires, thoughts, hopes or dreams" (Ephesians 3:20, Amplified).

Life doesn't always dish out what we expect. But if we remain open to new possibilities, the road ahead can be an adventure. It may be different than planned, the scenery may not be what we would have chosen, but it can be very, very good indeed. One way or another, God will get us to our final destination in glory.

And then…*every expectation we've ever had will fall absurdly short of Reality.*

CHAPTER TWENTY

ISLAND TREASURES

He will be the sure foundation for your times,
a rich store of salvation and wisdom and knowledge;
the fear of the Lord is the key to this treasure.

ISAIAH 33:6

The spring after Nathan was born, John and I were invited to the island of Kauai by our good friends Steve and Kathy. They have a beautiful home overlooking a valley, five minutes from the beach. For the last ten years we have found their home and their friendship to be safe and refreshing.

When we landed in Kauai, they told us all about special meetings their church was having while we were there. John and I glanced at each other. The last thing we wanted to do in Hawaii was "go to meetings." We'd escaped to Hawaii to get *away* from meetings, to rest, to play, to heal, to walk on the beach. We cringed at their announcement and schemed a way to diplomatically decline.

It didn't fly.

They were set on us going with them. So rather than offend them, we went.

The meeting was held in an elementary school cafeteria. Have you ever seen a padded cafeteria bench? They don't exist. It was 93 degrees in the building, 70 percent humidity, and the room had one pitifully tiny fan up in the far left corner. John and I were playing pass-the-cranky-baby game and whispering in unison, "Are we having fun yet?"

The singing went on for nearly an hour. Every time they repeated another verse John and I exchanged glances which said, *We ain't gettin' outta here till midnight!*

Finally the guest speaker, a lady, stepped up to the podium. John and I sighed in relief, knowing we were at least on the home stretch. She opened to the Book of Jeremiah and began to teach about the Potter and His lump of clay.

Just that quickly, God commanded our attention.

We forgot all about the heat, the humidity, and the unpadded benches. If Nathan fussed after that, neither of us remembers. It was as though the Holy Spirit stood up inside us and like a good coach said, "Listen up! We're going to learn something new tonight!"

That was an understatement.

Toward the end of the evening the speaker pointed to various people in the audience and encouraged them by quoting specific verses of Scripture to them. We didn't know anyone there, and they didn't know us, but it was evident that the Spirit of God was doing a beautiful, refreshing work in the hearts of those gathered on that warm, tropical evening.

And then she looked at us.

"That young couple back there," she said. "Would you please come down to the front and join me?"

The "young" part I liked. The "come down front" part I didn't. We probably would have protested had it not been for an advanced case of posterior numbing.

Keep in mind, this speaker didn't know us, and we didn't know her—or anyone else in the building except Kathy and Steve. They hadn't met the speaker or talked with her either. When we reached the front, she smiled, looked John straight in the eye, and began to speak Scriptures and word pictures to him.

And just like that, John started weeping.

We both did. She spoke to John about his discouragement and his secret thoughts of leaving the ministry. (Grief has a knack for evoking irrational thoughts.) She encouraged him to be faithful to his calling. She didn't know who she was talking to, but God did. And He had moved us to the front of the room so we didn't miss a single word.

Then she turned to me. "Your son almost died at birth," she said, "but he lived because God wanted him to live. So...don't worry."

That did it. Now I was standing in puddles. She had cut right to the heart of my struggle with all those pesky "What if's." *What if he has to go through open heart surgery? What if I don't have what it takes to raise a handicapped child? What if the stress is too much on the other children?* I smiled back at her through my tears and told her I would try not to worry.

With eyes of compassion she said, "There is a big difference, you know, between worry and intercessory prayer."

Bottom line: *Quit fretting, and start praying!*

We left Kauai a week later with more than seashells in our pockets. There were spiritual treasures there, too. Treasures from the hand of God. John's vision for ministry was restored, and I made more room in my life for prayer. Yes, some days I felt like I was only "going through the motions," but I knew it didn't matter. God's ability to answer prayer isn't influenced by how we *feel*.

After we got back home, I began turning to Scripture in a way I hadn't done for a long time. I would read a passage, then repeat it back to the Lord in the form of a prayer. One passage I especially remember is the first three verses of Isaiah 61. I recognized it as a prophetic passage about the earthly ministry of Jesus Christ. But it also has a message for our lives *right now.*

> The Spirit of the Sovereign Lord is on me,
> because the Lord has anointed me
> to preach good news to the poor.
> He has sent me to bind up the brokenhearted,
> to proclaim freedom for the captives
> release from darkness for the prisoners,
> to proclaim the year of the Lord's favor
> and the day of vengeance of our God,
> to comfort all who mourn,
> and provide for those who grieve in Zion—
> to bestow on them a crown of beauty
> instead of ashes,
> the oil of gladness
> instead of mourning,
> a garment of praise
> instead of a spirit of despair.
> They will be called oaks of righteousness,
> a planting of the Lord
> for the display of his splendor.

I made these verses my own and prayed something like this:

God, thank You that You have good news for the poor. I'M the one who is poor in spirit today. I'M the one who needs good news. MY heart needs to be healed. Nathan's does, too. God, would You please touch his heart and mend the holes? And God, I know You can set captives free. Well, I'M the captive right now. Please free me from faulty thinking and fears of what tomorrow may bring. Please push back the darkness in my soul and comfort me.

This verse says You will provide for those who grieve. I'M the one who needs Your provision today. I need You to replace any residue of mourning with gladness and joy. By the power of Your mighty Spirit, please disrobe the despair I'm feeling and replace it with a garment of praise.

This verse says that You are the One who does the bestowing. Would You please do that for me today? Let my roots go down deep in You so that I'm planted strong and firm, able to weather whatever today brings my way.

God knew in advance that we would have difficult times in this world. Christ told His disciples, "In the world you *will* have tribulation." It's a given. It comes with our membership card for the human race. The only people without problems are those without a pulse. And with a full understanding of those hard times, God says in Isaiah 61 that He has made provision for us so that we don't have to get stuck or arrested in our grief.

God is a gentleman; He won't force Himself upon us. He'll wait patiently for us to open our hearts and invite Him in. John and I could have closed our ears in that stuffy cafeteria that night. We could have flown away from Hawaii with empty pockets and empty hearts.

Instead, we came away with treasure. And our Father was well pleased. It was what He'd planned all along.

CHAPTER TWENTY-ONE

THE VALENTINE

I have called upon You, for You will hear me, O God;
incline Your ear to me....
Show Your marvelous lovingkindness by Your right hand,
O You who save those who trust in You....
Keep me as the apple of Your eye;
hide me under the shadow of Your wings.
PSALM 17:6–8, NKJV

My friend Launi is a single mom with a darling six-year-old girl.

Years ago, Launi had walked down the aisle like many of the rest of us, with sparkling eyes and a heart bursting with hopes and dreams. Her Prince Charming was the perfect match, an answer to prayer.

That was the "before" picture. I've known Launi in the "after" years.

Seems her prince fell off his white horse and started frequenting bars and other off-color joints. Before she knew it, she was catching angry fists, wondering what hit her. It was a horrible nightmare, but it didn't end at sunup. It just went on and on. And then...he was gone.

Never in Launi's wildest dreams did she imagine being abandoned and forced to leave the home she loved.

Launi and little Kelsey had to find a place to start over.

The new apartment was small but peaceful. A far cry better

than having a lot of room in a battle zone! Launi worked long hours to hang on to that little spot they now called "home." But when the first of the month rolled around one dark winter day, she realized it just wasn't going to work. Her money wasn't going to stretch far enough to pay the rent. This single mom was battle worn, angry, and—need I say it?—deeply frightened.

"God," she prayed, "I just can't take it anymore. I didn't ask for *any* of this! I've lost my home, my marriage, and my dreams. And now I can't even pay the rent."

Ten tissues later, Launi plodded into the kitchen to rehearse her options for the umpteenth time. It didn't help. It rarely does. The dark times have a way of driving our ruminations; we review and review, forgetting that God sees it all.

Next stop? Sunday morning church. Now that *did* help, because one point Pastor Roberts made stuck with her: "Ask God for something specific, and let Him prove His love to you."

Rising to that challenge, Launi asked God for rent money. The next day her apartment manager gave her a seventy-two hour eviction notice! Not quite the answer she'd anticipated from God. Life is like that. Sometimes things get worse before they get better.

Sobbing into her pillow, Launi cried, "I'm afraid! I don't want to move. Kelsey likes this place. We just got settled here. What am I going to do?"

On Valentine's Day, Launi rose at first light, sat down at the kitchen table, and wrote a letter:

Dear Jesus,
I believe You love Kelsey and me. I believe You wrote us a
Valentine and signed it with Your own blood when You died

on the cross. I have done all I know to do. If You can part the Red Sea and heal the sick, then there has to be a way You can help us. If You want me to do something, tell me, and I will do it.

Love, Your daughter,
Launi

In the quietness of her heart, she sensed the Lord say one little word.

"*Wait.*"

She realized that she was not to do another thing. She wasn't to try to figure it out or come up with a plan. She was to wait.

Wanting to prepare Kelsey for possible changes, Launi held her girl on her lap and with uncharacteristic courage said, "Kelsey, I don't know if we are going to be living here much longer. There isn't enough money to pay the rent, and the manager may make us move. But God is going to take care of us no matter where we are."

As those words left her mouth, the phone rang. It was a friend from her Bible study.

"Do you have your rent money this month?" she asked.

"Well—no," Launi said, totally off guard.

"My husband is a barber," the woman continued, "and he has a little tin can on his dresser where he keeps tidbits of his daily earnings. The can hasn't been emptied for a while, but he felt compelled to get up at three this morning to count the ones, fives, and tens. We want you to have it. No strings attached. There's four hundred dollars for you."

Just try to guess the rent payment. *Four hundred dollars even!* Not a penny more, not a penny less.

When Launi told her daughter the good news, Kelsey

exclaimed with glee, "Mama, we just have to go to God when we need help, don't we?"

There's a little girl and a single mom in Gresham, Oregon, who were forced to release so much of what they had known and loved. Life still isn't easy for them. But it's better. Much better. And if you were to share some heart-shaped cookies and milk around their kitchen table, you can be sure you'd hear about Heaven's valentine…that came in a barber's tin can.

I'm not sure what this story says to you, but to me the message couldn't be much more pointed: Turn to God. Quit running elsewhere. Quit grasping. Quit striving. The psalmist captured these words from the Lord: "Be still, and know that I am God" (Psalm 46:10). Solomon put it another way:

> Trust in the LORD with all your heart; do not depend on your own understanding. Seek his will in all you do, and he will direct your paths. (Proverbs 3:5–6, NLT)

That's a valentine that's even better than chocolates.

CHAPTER TWENTY-TWO

Memorial Day

People should think of us as servants of Christ,
the ones God has trusted with his secrets.
1 Corinthians 4:1, NCV

Determination. Destination. Overdrive.

These are the masculine principles that prevail when it's time to leave for a family vacation. I have come to believe that the top priority for those of the male species is "getting there." Forget fun little shops, historical markers, or interesting roadside attractions. Forget lengthy potty stops, too. Better yet, *hold it*. And count on the usual baritone comments along the way like, "For cryin' out loud! That guy in front of us is going forty-five in the *passing* lane!"

Memorial Day Weekend was no different.

John was steely determined to get "our spot" for the camper on the Deschutes River. Convinced that most of Oregon (and half of California) would try to snag our favorite site, he decided to beat the crowds and leave a day early. So he and the boys beat a trail over Mt. Hood Thursday night and waited for Jessie and me to join them the next day after fulfilling some Friday morning commitments in town. It's a man thing.

The weekend, however, was relaxed. We sat around the campfire, poking embers and feasting on more toasty marshmallows than our stomachs could comfortably hold. (I now believe that S'more hangovers do exist.) Our days were filled with mountain biking the trails, horseback riding, fishing, catching garter snakes, and some fierce card games of "War" and "Old Maid" after dark.

The kids skunked us every time. After rubbing it in, they climbed into our bunk for bedtime stories. That's right. Five of us packed ourselves into that "queen size" bunk (designed for a very petite queen) like a family of five sardines, and we fed our spirits from a children's book a friend had given us the day we left for camping. *Somewhere Angels* has become a family favorite.

When the minivacation was over, John and I made a vow. We will *never* travel home on Memorial Day again. Stop-and-go traffic on the highway from Bend to Portland turned a three-hour scenic trip into a five-and-a-half-hour endurance marathon.

This time, Nathan and I followed the camper in the car. Jessie and Ben snoozed their way through the congestion while John tried to keep his mind on more positive things than the bumper in front of him. After an hour and twenty minutes of creeping along at ten miles an hour, the traffic finally cleared, and the speedometer hit fifty-five again.

Nathan was quiet most of the trip. He surprised me when he suddenly broke the silence with, "Mama, Mama!" while clasping his hands together in front of him. He was telling me in his sign language that he wanted me to pray.

"All right, Nathan," I said. "Who do you want me to pray for?"

"Nnnn," came the reply.

That's Nathan's word for Andrew, the little boy up the street who plays with Ben now and then.

So I prayed for Andrew. I asked God to bless him and his family.

Then Nathan clasped his hands again and asked me to pray for Jessie.

Then Ben. Then Dad. Then Mama. Then Grandma and Grandpa. After praying at length for the entire family, I figured we were done. Not according to Nathan! My little copilot kept giving me the "pray" sign with his hands clasped tightly together, followed by adamant pointing to our camper in front of us.

"Nathan," I explained, "Mommy *already* prayed for Daddy and Jessie and Ben."

Irritated, he again gave me the "pray" sign and pointed to the camper.

What in the world did he want? What was on his heart? I could tell he felt very strongly about what he was trying to communicate.

So I made some guesses.

"Nathan, do you want me to pray for Daddy?"

"No."

"Jessie?"

"No."

"Ben?"

"No."

He kept pointing to the *camper*. Insistently! I gave it one more try. "Nathan, do you want me to pray for the camper?"

"Da!" (Nathan's version of "yes")

I thought the request a bit strange, but I accommodated him and prayed that God would take care of the camper and keep it in good working condition all the way home.

After I said "amen," Nathan relaxed and seemed happy, and that was that.

A few breaths later we rounded a curve, crested a hill, and had to slam on our breaks to avoid hitting our camper, which suddenly skidded wildly to a stop in front of us. John and I had descended upon an accident that had happened just moments before. A truck pulling a large horse trailer had crashed into a motor home that stopped abruptly for another car crossing its lane. The force of the impact lifted the rear of the motor home off the ground and spun it around, leaving it in the lane of oncoming traffic. The right front wheel had popped off, and the motor home was tilted to the side. Smoke rolled across the highway in clouds. Injured passengers scrambled out of damaged vehicles to get out of danger.

The people in the car in front of us pulled flares from their trunks, dialed their cell phones, checked the injured, and directed traffic.

I just sat there, stunned.

I couldn't believe what I was seeing. It so easily could have been us! Our whole family. Minutes before John and I had been the ones in front of the truck pulling the horses.

I'm not sure I understand the connection between Nathan's insistence that I pray specifically for the camper and our protection on the road that day.

But I do believe there was a connection.

Some might call it discernment. Others, spiritual perception. All I know is that Nathan sensed something and worked very hard to get me to pray. I like to think he was being a faithful steward of the mysteries of God (1 Corinthians 4:1).

Nathan has taught us many lessons since his arrival, but one dominates in my mind as I reflect on the moments that preceded that accident on Memorial Day: *Life is full of mystery.* So much is unknown and undetected by our five senses. Many important questions do not have answers. Not everything folds up nicely into tidy, geometric boxes. But healing comes as I move away from rigidity and learn to tolerate mystery, ambiguity, and uncertainty. Worship happens as I bow before my heavenly Father with the recognition that the more I know Him, the more I really don't know.

Perhaps that's what Paul had in mind when he said, "Oh, the depth of the riches both of the wisdom and knowledge of God! How unsearchable are His judgments and unfathomable His ways!" (Romans 11:33, NASB).

That's a fancy, theological way of saying, "I don't really get it, but it doesn't matter...because *He* does."

CHAPTER TWENTY-THREE

THE GIFT OF LETTING GO

Cast your burden upon the LORD,
and He will sustain you;
He will never allow the righteous to be shaken.
PSALM 55:22, NASB

Billy Graham tells a story about a small boy caught playing with an extremely valuable vase. The little guy had put his hand into it but couldn't take it out! His father tried his best to help him but all in vain.

They were thinking gloomily of breaking the beautiful vase when the father sighed and said, "Now Son, make one more try. Open your hand, and hold your fingers out straight as you see me doing, and then *pull*."

To their astonishment the little fellow said, "Oh no, Father. I couldn't put my fingers out like that. Because if I did, I'd drop my penny!"[1]

Smile if you will—but thousands of us are like that little boy, so busy holding on to the world's worthless penny that we cannot accept liberation.

Try a little exercise with me. I'd like you to clench your fist into a ball, squeeze as hard as you possibly can, and count to ten. Ready? *Go.* S-Q-U-E-E-E-E-Z-E.

Okay, relax now. How did your fist feel, gripped so tightly like that? What did it look like? Can you describe the sensations you felt? How did it feel to release your grip and open your hand after the ten-count?

When your hand was clenched, it was uncomfortable, wasn't it? Tight. Tense. Bloodless. Unable to move freely. Not only that, it wasn't able to do what it was *designed* to do. It was closed, unable to receive. But when you let go and opened your hand, you could feel the blood returning to your fingers, couldn't you? Your hand became warm again. The discomfort left, and your hand felt relief. Your fingers moved naturally... and were in a much better position to receive!

Similarities can be found between our physical body and our psyche. When we walk through life, grasping, clinging, clutching, and desperately trying to hang on to things that should naturally be released, we ache. We hurt. We become emotionally constricted and locked up in pain. We get tied up in knots. We lose movement in our lives and feel paralyzed.

I like what one person said about letting go: "If you love something, set it free. If it comes back, you didn't lose it. If it doesn't come back, you never owned it to start with. If it just sits there watching TV, unaware that you ever set it free, you probably married it!"

None of us enjoy losses. Our world system conditions us to avoid loss at all costs. We don't like to let go of something we treasure, love, value, or own. When we have to let go, it usually ends up with claw marks all over it!

A while back I surveyed more than two hundred people and asked them this question: "What are you finding difficult to let go of at this time in your life?" These are a few of the answers I received:

I am finding it hard to let go of...
my kindergartener heading off to school

my parents, because they didn't want to let go of me
my childhood dreams, because I realize they aren't realistic
anymore
a friendship that went sour
shame from my past
the baby we lost to SIDS
a job I loved and lost due to downsizing
my marriage
a bad habit I can't seem to break
my teenager who has gone astray
my freedom, my sleep, and my body, as I recently became a
  new mom
my youth

Whether we like it or not, life brings us face to face with people, situations, feelings, and objects that we must release, for our own good. Little deaths come our way.

Empty spaces.

Holes.

And so do feelings of grief. When we are grieving these losses, it helps to know that God has good counsel for us. He hasn't left us hanging. Solomon penned these lovely lines—and it is so much more than poetry!

There is a time for everything,
  a season for every activity under heaven.
A time to be born and a time to die.
  A time to plant and a time to harvest.
A time to kill and a time to heal.
  A time to tear down and a time to rebuild.
A time to cry and a time to laugh.
  A time to grieve and a time to dance.

A time to scatter stones and a time to gather stones.
    A time to embrace and a time to turn away.
A time to search and a time to lose.
    A time to keep and a time to throw away.
A time to tear and a time to mend.
    A time to be quiet and a time to speak up.
A time to love and a time to hate.
    A time for war and a time for peace....
God has made everything beautiful for its own time.
He has planted eternity in the human heart.

(Ecclesiastes 3:1–8,11, NLT)

God has made everything beautiful in its time. Even the empty spaces. Even the holes. Now that's a hard concept for me to believe when I am frantically grasping the last few strands of whatever is trying to escape my clutches. The pain involved in letting go does not feel "beautiful" to me...it feels downright miserable.

The New Testament tells us that in God's economy, new life springs forth from death. Death is the secret of fruitfulness. Jesus tried to help His followers understand this. His disciples had seen His triumphs. They had witnessed His miracles and experienced His power in their midst. They felt confident in their hearts that He would soon establish His kingdom on earth.

One afternoon Jesus sat down on a hillside and told them that the time had come for Him to be glorified—but *not* in the manner in which they expected. It was to be by His death. With tenderness and feeling, Christ wove them an illustration:

"The time has come for the Son of Man to be glorified. Listen carefully: Unless a grain of wheat is buried in the ground, dead to the world, it is never any more than a

grain of wheat. But if it is buried, it sprouts and repro-
duces itself many times over. In the same way, anyone
who *holds on to life* just as it is destroys that life. But if
you *let it go*, reckless in your love, you'll have it forever,
real and eternal.... Right now I am storm-tossed. And
what am I going to say? 'Father, get me out of this'? No,
this is why I came in the first place. I'll say, 'Father, *put
your glory on display*.'" (John 12:23–25, 27–28, *The
Message*, emphasis mine)

Death is the secret of fruitfulness, and Jesus explains the
process: No death, no germination. No germination, no fruit.
No fruit, no beauty. For Christ, the analogy was very personal.
His death was to become the gateway to life. Without His
death there would be no resurrection...*for any of us.*

The message is personal for you and me, too. It's a message of
hope when life steals from us and leaves us with empty arms. It's
a message of strength when we're stripped bare and it feels like
we're facing the future empty-handed. It's a message of substance
that can fill the holes in our soul with promise. God says to us:

WHEN YOU ARE LETTING GO, REMEMBER THAT I
AM PLANTING SEEDS OF NEW LIFE IN YOU. YOUR
GRIEF IS ONLY FOR A SEASON. MY END IS NOT
DEATH. IT IS *ALWAYS* LIFE. I AM THE AUTHOR OF
LIFE.[2]

These are the promises we have to hang on to when we are
doing the hard work of letting go. And letting go is certainly
hard work. It is often very confusing and bewildering. To break
away from someone or something that we have been bonded
to rips our emotions. It goes against our natural instincts to

break bonds. The parting cannot happen without inward bleeding. The greater the bond, the greater the pain.

Our head and our heart are usually in conflict. Our head says: "This is what I need to do for my own good. Move on. I need to let go because God is telling me to let go. I need to let go for the sake of my kids, or my spouse, or the friendship, or my own growth and development." But our heart says: "Oh no you don't! It hurts too much. I can't do it. I *won't* do it!" Our logic and our emotions war with one another.

Letting go is a process, not an instantaneous event. It starts with an awareness that we *need* to let go. When our awareness increases, our pain increases. I saw a poster that described the process perfectly. The cartoon depicted a woman with her head and arms being squeezed through the wringers of an old washing machine. Anguish covered her face. The caption read: "The truth will set you free…but first it will make you miserable."

I remember the aches in my empty arms after I delivered our first baby who died halfway to term. With postpartum hormones raging, the grief was more than I wanted to endure. I was at the counseling center one morning and said to my colleague, "I wish I could take a pill that would make these feelings go away."

He was very kind and like a good friend spoke the truth in love: "I can sure understand that, Pam. *But then you would just have to work through your grief later.*"

He made a point which I understand more fully now. When we are feeling our pain, we are progressing. We tend to get that mixed up. We think that if we feel pain deeply, we are "losing it," or cracking up, or getting ready to check in to the Funny Farm. Nothing is further from the truth! When we are feeling, we are progressing through the grief process.

Fish swim…birds fly…*and people feel.*

Feeling is healing.

Letting go demands we feel and ride out our grief. If we deny, stuff, or numb ourselves, we end up camping out in our grief…and never progress beyond it. We cut ourselves off from the treasures God has hidden for us in the empty spaces.

What do we need to do? You already know the answer in your heart. We need to turn to the Lord our God.

It sounds so basic, but when we're in pain, our first tendency is often to retreat from everyone, including God. We run in all kinds of directions, keeping ourselves excessively busy. We turn to activities, food, alcohol, novels, shopping, entertainment, and other people to mask our pain.

In our times of letting go, God is the One we need to run to, because He knows us better than we know ourselves. He is the Specialist who can give us insight into our needs. He is the Chief Guide who can offer direction when we are confused. He's the Caretaker of our souls who can give us strength and courage when we are afraid to let go.

In the midst of our pain we need to run to God and say, "God, I need Your help. Give me Your perspective. Let my eyes see as You see. Let my heart hear Your heart. What do You want to accomplish in my life right now? Show me what I need to do to cooperate with You in my healing."

And then, dear friend, pay very close attention to the people the Lord brings across your path and the situations that present themselves. Because God will be faithful to answer those kinds of prayers…and to put His glory on display.

In you.

CHAPTER TWENTY-FOUR

A Snap of the Fingers

Teach us to number our days aright,
that we may gain a heart of wisdom.
PSALM 90:12

John and I are sometimes stopped in our tracks by the realization that what we say and do when we're with Jessie, Ben, and Nathan may become part of their memories for a *lifetime*.

Childhood memories are either a source of enduring treasure through the years or an area of our minds we never willingly visit again. Count my reminiscences on the "treasure" side of the ledger. That's what John and I want for our children, too. We realize that childhood years click by like a snap of the fingers. And as the Lord enables us, we want to create the kind of loving atmosphere in our home that is conducive to happy memories. Beyond that, we want our vacations and family fun times to weave recollections of new places, faces, and experiences—hopefully blended with healthy doses of togetherness and laughter.

But as we all know, the truly memorable times don't always flow out of planned activities and scheduled events. Life has a habit of simply "coming at you," doesn't it? And when you are the parent of a special needs child, it often comes at you more rapidly than you can readily process. You have to simply lean on the Spirit of God and try to *respond* as He leads.

Ironically, those may be the very moments we later call "unforgettable."

Nathan provided the material for such an occasion on our last trip south. As it turned out, our youngest brought a total stranger to our door early one morning. And that stranger gave us a message we will never forget. But I'm getting ahead of myself. Here's how the story unfolded....

Around about December, the Oregon rain and gloom has a way of turning even the most lighthearted Pollyanna's into grumpy old geezers. So this year we decided to package some sunshine therapy into our Christmas vacation with a trip to Palm Springs.

We had heard about this particular RV resort from some friends, and it turned out to be everything we were hoping for. There were about a thousand mobile homes and RV sites in the resort. The crystal clear ponds were stocked full of fish for little boys and girls to reel in with delight. Elegant black swans roamed the manicured lawns while families played tennis, basketball, Ping-Pong, pool, horseshoes, and shuffleboard. We enjoyed making the rounds of all the activities but the Vredevelts are known for being pool hogs. We melted our coating of Northwest frost by basking in the warmth of the sun and soaking our bones in a pool fed by natural desert hot springs.

John and I thought we were pretty clever taking the kids to the hot tub right before bedtime. We figured we could "boil" the ants out of their pants, and then we would all sleep better—and hopefully longer.

At Grandma and Grandpa's the week before, Nathan had toddled his way to Grandpa's side of the bed each morning around 6:00 A.M. He wanted his pal to share some Cheerios and toast while watching the sunrise. Grandpa's breakfast routine was a ministry of mercy to Nathan's vacation-minded parents.

But Grandpa wasn't in Palm Springs, and John and I dreaded

the thought of a shrill 6:00 A.M. alarm that spouted, "Mama! Dada! Mama! Dada!" We just wanted to sleep in…a little. I told the Lord I'd be grateful if He could just give us until 7:30 A.M.

Well, God has a way of answering prayers…but not always in the way you might anticipate.

We were all deep in our slumbers when someone startled us awake by pounding on our camper door. Ben jumped up and went to see who was outside. He flipped the lock, opened the door, and the next thing I heard was an older man's voice saying, "Do you folks have a little boy who is missing?"

That got me out of my blankets.

I rubbed my eyes and caught a half-focused view of Nathan's bed. Empty! Bolting to the door in my pajamas, hair wigged out every which way, I faced a kind-looking gentleman with Nathan in tow. Our little boy was wearing his fuzzy pajama sleeper, no shoes, and a proud smile that seemed to say, "Hey Mom, I found a new friend!"

I thanked Nathan's rescuer over and over. I had at least two reasons to hug Nathan tightly to my chest: one, out of sheer relief that he was all right and two, out of embarrassment that I was standing in front of a complete stranger in my silk jammies!

I said a quick good-bye to the man at the door and brought Nathan inside. Questions darted between us. How did he get out? How long had he been gone? Who was that man who brought him back? How had he known Nathan belonged to us?

Our worst nightmare had happened. Nathan had been lost—and we hadn't even known it! When we asked Nathan how he got out, he pointed to some sliding windows. He had maneuvered the windows just enough to slip through the crack and venture out on his escapade. None of us had heard a thing.

We calmed our nerves with some pancakes and eggs and then gathered our towels to go to the pool. That's when the Great Escape story began to unfold. A sweet elderly woman in the mobile home across from our rig stopped us with a few of the details.

"Your little boy came over about 7:00 A.M. and knocked on our door," she told us. "When I opened it, he made a beeline for the bedroom, jumped in my bed, and told me in sign language that he wanted to go to sleep. I had a dickens of a time trying to get him out of bed!

"I didn't know who he belonged to, so I walked him around the park for an hour. Then he just took off lickety-split down the road. Just like that," she said with a finger snap. "Poof! He was gone."

Her next comment caught me completely off guard. "I'm a Canadian," she said, "and I really don't want to get involved in American affairs, so I just let him go."

My jaw about hit the pavement. *Let him go?* I couldn't believe it! She let a little child wander and calmly walked back to her mobile home—just because she didn't want to "get involved"? This was a little boy we were talking about, not someone's lost car keys!

I bridled my responses, thanked her for walking Nathan around the park for an hour, and apologized for the intrusion. Before we parted, I asked her if she happened to know the man who brought him home to us. No, she said quickly, she hadn't seen a thing. (And probably hadn't *wanted* to see a thing.)

We enjoyed our sunny morning by the pool. The kids were hot-tubbing and John and I were absorbed in some good books when a voice suddenly boomed behind us.

"How's that little boy of yours doing?"

I turned around to see Nathan's beaming rescuer. After

proper introductions, he filled in the blanks of our son's early morning adventures.

Al had been sitting in his motor home reading the paper when something caught his eye. Peeking over the daily news he saw a barefooted toddler dart by in fuzzy red pajamas. But something was obviously wrong with that picture. There were no parents chasing the little guy.

He startled his wife by saying, "I think there's a little boy outside who has escaped. I'm going to check it out."

By the time Al got outside, Nathan was nearly to the end of the street—and Al wasn't quite in shape for a hundred-yard dash. Seeing an eight-year-old boy on a bicycle at the stop sign, Al called out, "Hey Sonny—when that little boy gets to the stop sign, hang onto him for me. I'll be there quick as I can."

Joshua, the little boy, hopped off his bike, and held his arms open wide. Nathan laughed and ran right into his bear hug.

The three of them shared a friendly powwow out there in the street (while Mom and Dad Vredevelt slept blissfully on)! Then Al and Nathan walked hand in hand around the park. "Take me to your mommy and daddy," Al said. Nathan eagerly led the way, getting down on his hands and knees and crawling under a hedgerow of arborvitae. Al shrugged his shoulders and plunged under the hedge after him. When the two emerged from the dirt and brush, Nathan pointed over to the next street where our camper was parked. Moments later, Al knocked on our door.

Al and his wife, Judy, we learned, were "veterans." They had a daughter who was severely brain damaged at birth. When she was seven years old, they could no longer meet her needs at home and had to place her in a full-care medical facility. Forty years had passed since then, but tears welled up in Al's eyes as if it had all happened yesterday.

Pretty heavy poolside chat.

We thanked our Palm Springs grandpa again and again for his kindness. He started to walk away with a wave of the hand, but then turned back.

"Nathan is a love," he said softly. "You take good care of him and enjoy him…while you have him. Someday you may have to give him up, and that'll be very hard on you."

Of the hundreds of people in the RV resort that week, Nathan "just happened" to cross paths with a grandpa and grandma who knew how to relate to youngsters with special needs. Intercepting our little escape artist, they shielded him from harm and danger. I shudder to think what could have happened with all the inviting ponds and swimming pools around. Ah, but I'm learning that ruminating on the "what ifs" wastes the precious time and energy I need for my family.

So I'll stick to the facts.

Everything turned out all right. And the Lord taught us some lessons along the way. Our senior friend reminded us of the brevity of life and the limited time we have to make special memories with our children. In a few short years we'll be snapping our fingers saying, "It's like our kids were here one minute and gone the next."

When it comes to building memories, we can't do anything about yesterday, and tomorrow is beyond our reach. But *today*…today is a commodity we can work with.

By His grace and in His kindness, we will.

CHAPTER TWENTY-FIVE

A PATH AROUND THE SWAMP

You intended to harm me,
but God intended it for good,
to accomplish what is now being done,
the saving of many lives.
GENESIS 50:20

Mom is one of God's Medal of Honor winners. She's not in the public eye, campaigning on the front lines for causes and cures. But make no mistake, her contributions are applauded in the grandstands of heaven. They are quiet, unassuming acts of kindness.

One of Mom's greatest gifts is her listening ear. Not pat answers. Not analysis. Not advice. Not even Scripture verses. But an open, receptive heart. Her silent care *heals*. It's a safe place to sort things out.

A shelter.

But how in the world did she come by such grace and patience?

It certainly didn't come from any home environment. You see, Mom didn't grow up with the blessings she has given me. She's been the recipient of some of life's greatest heartaches. When she was six months old and her brother was just eighteen months old, her mother simply walked out of the house and never looked back. They never saw her again.

On naval duty in China, Mom's father received word that

his wife had initiated divorce proceedings and was leaving them. The children were kept by friends until their father made arrangements for them to go to their grandparents in Arkansas.

The early memories with Grandma and Grandpa Dalton are warm but dim. Mom remembers a few golden moments—just a taste, a flicker, of happy childhood. When she was almost four, life took another abrupt turn. Her father remarried, and she and her brother went to live with a new mother and a father who was absent much of the time. As a military family, they uprooted constantly. During that pre-World War II era many naval families moved several times a year, as did Mom's family. It was all part of defending our country. War has many costs, and this was one. They never stayed long enough in one place for a lonely little girl to find and hold many friendships. Who can measure a quiet child's loneliness and secret sorrows? Who can quantify the pain?

But Mom made significant choices along the way…decisions that shaped her life and, as a result, *my* life—and so many others.

She reminds me of the story in Matthew 18:21–22, where Peter says to Jesus, "Lord, how many times shall I forgive my brother when he sins against me? Up to seven times?" And Jesus answered, "I tell you, not seven times, but seventy times seven." When I was growing up, I watched my mother extend herself in loving ways to our family, extended family, and friends. It wasn't until my late twenties that she told me about some of her childhood wounds. I remember walking away from that conversation shaking my head in amazement. I was flabbergasted. I still am. She's miles ahead of me in mastering the art of forgiveness.

Perhaps that is what enabled her to break the patterns of

the generation before her. Mom's birth mother left her with a legacy of abandonment, divorce, and abuse.

But Mom did it differently.

She chose to maintain her commitment to her husband and children through the good and the bad. Rather than divorce, she became her husband's best friend and partner in life. Rather than abuse, she chose to raise their children in an environment of discipline tempered with love, kindness, and respect. It would have been *so easy* for Mom to have nurtured the "if only's" in her life. There were a good many of them! But somehow, by God's grace, she chose a different road.

We do ourselves a favor to follow suit, because the "if only's" of life lead us down a winding path into uncertain, even dangerous swampy areas. Wading through such boggy ground can pull at our feet, making it hard to move.

Or it can swallow you up completely.

One of those quagmires is called "blame." Stay on the "if only" path long enough, and you'll get there.

The blame game sounds like this: "If only so-and-so hadn't done such-and-such, then I would have…" You fill in the blank. Between the lines, blame is attached to another person. When we blame others, we get stuck in anger and bitterness. Some who have wandered into this swamp never leave.

I've noticed something about human nature. Many of us attribute the cause of our anger and pain to other people or situations. I hear comments from clients like:

- "If my wife kept a clean house, I wouldn't get so ticked-off."
- "If my kids would just do what I tell 'em to, I wouldn't get angry."
- "If my boss wouldn't ride me the way he does—or

assign me so many projects—I wouldn't have a short fuse."

Can you see what that kind of thinking does? It keeps our sights locked onto *others* being the problem. We give them more control than they deserve! It's as though we hand them a book of matches to light our fuse.

Victor Frankl, in his classic work *Man's Search for Meaning*, recounts his days in Nazi death camps during World War Two. He tells the stories of prisoners who seemed to rise above the horrific conditions of the camp, while others were utterly crushed by them.

Frankl concluded that the critical difference was based on *inner choice*, not outside conditions. Those who survived did so because of the meaning they chose to find within their souls as they endured the hardships of the camp. Rather than giving the prison guards or the atrocities of the death camp power over them, they chose to turn life into an inner triumph. Rather than blaming others and believing death was just around the corner, they chose to believe God would give them life. Rather than limiting their focus to cause and effect, they chose to believe there were reasons beyond reason. [1]

You and I aren't in wartime, nor are we confined to a concentration camp. Be we have our own set of problems and choices. Finding meaning in our difficulties is necessary for survival. It's far more important than skills, talents, intelligence, or change of circumstances. In God's kingdom, meaning can always be found in suffering. It is meaning that sustains us through deep disappointments and allows us to perceive His-appointments.

Recently I spoke with a pastor and his wife about some of the hardships they had suffered in ministry. Pastor Tim was an assistant pastor at a large church for a number of years. He enjoyed his relationships on staff and was effective in ministry. But after several years of service, he began sensing confusing signals from the senior pastor.

Tim and his wife explained the situation to John and me over dinner one night. "It was strange," he told us. "It was a Dr. Jekyll-Mr. Hyde situation. Sometimes when we talked to him we felt affirmed and respected. But at other times we felt a cold wall between us. After several months of this, we were asked to find a position elsewhere."

When Tim tried to dialogue with the senior pastor about this abrupt turn of events, the older man would only give them vague, inconclusive replies. Tim left that church never understanding what went wrong or why he lost his job.

Several years later, after Tim was well established in another ministry, the phone in his office rang. He picked up the receiver and recognized the voice of his former senior pastor on the line. He wanted to talk with Tim about his dismissal.

Apparently another staff member, whom I'll call Martin, had been feeding the pastor subtle lies about Tim. It was all shared "in confidence" so the pastor never discussed those things with Tim. But he did form an opinion!

A couple of years after Tim and his family had moved on, however, the senior pastor caught Martin in a lie and confronted him. One lie unraveled many other lies...and the truth finally came out. Martin had been jealous of Tim and set out on a campaign to get rid of him. As the lies were exposed, the senior pastor realized what a terrible mistake he had made in asking Tim to leave.

Over the telephone this broken older man said, "Tim, the doctors have given me three months to live, and I need to make things right with you. Can you ever forgive me for believing the lies?"

Tim and his wife were clearly the victims of someone else's wrongs. In moments of despair, they blamed the senior pastor for rejecting them without explanation or dialogue. Nevertheless, God was sovereign and had His way in their lives. He moved them to a prominent place where their impact in ministry is now broader than ever.

What impressed me most about this seasoned couple was the faith they maintained through that painful ordeal. Wrapping up the story over dinner, they said that daily the Lord challenged them not to look back, point the finger, or blame. He challenged them to believe He was bigger than those who had mistreated them. He was bigger than the directives that had come from man. And He would faithfully accomplish His plans in their lives.

Out of raw discipline and sheer obedience, they chose to obey the voice of the Lord. They chose to believe in spite of the circumstances. I had the joy of meeting them years later, when the fulfillment of God's promises to them had come to pass.

Peter might have used these words to describe the experience of this godly couple:

Don't be bewildered or surprised when you go through the fiery trials ahead, for this is no strange, unusual thing that is going to happen to you. Instead, be really glad—because these trials will make you partners with Christ in his suffering, and afterwards you will have the wonderful joy of *sharing his glory*.... So if you are suffering according to God's will, keep on doing what is right and trust yourself to God who made you, for he will never fail you. (1 Peter 4:12–14, 19, *The Message*)

During times of suffering we are vulnerable to discouragement and attacks from the powers of darkness. Satan, the accuser, is the author of lies—and delights in them! Yet part of the reason Christ died on the cross was to destroy the works of the devil. Rest assured: God will have the final say in your life, if that is the dominant desire of your heart.

If my mom had chosen to name herself a victim and had pitched her tent in the swampy province of Point-and-Blame, could I have found her when heartache swept across my own life like a cold and withering wind? Would she have been there for me, a refuge in my sorrow?

Those questions don't really need an answer, because Mom skirted that swamp and stayed on the solid ground of Christ's provision.

She *has* been a shelter...quiet, strong, and good.

I want to be a shelter, too.

CHAPTER TWENTY-SIX

DID GOD MAKE
A MISTAKE?

The word of the LORD came to me, saying,
"Before I formed you in the womb I knew you,
before you were born I set you apart; I appointed you."
JEREMIAH 1:4–5

Lydia and her husband know all about unintentional errors.

She was telling me about a time when she and her husband were having lunch together. He pulled his white, no-frills handkerchief out of his back pocket, unfolded it, and vigorously blew his nose. After a few good snorts he folded the hanky corner to corner, crease to crease, and neatly slipped it into his back pocket.

He looked up and noticed her mouth gaping in surprise.

"What?" he said.

"Do you *always* fold your hanky like that after you've used it?" she asked.

"Well, yes, as a matter of fact I do," he replied. "Is that a problem for you?"

Lydia just shook her head. "After twenty-five years of marriage I had no idea that you folded your hanky like that after blowing your nose."

"Will you tell me why that's such a big deal?" he demanded.

"I'm sorry to tell you this," she said, "but when I'm doing the laundry and I find that hanky so neatly folded in your back pocket, I assume it hasn't been used. So I simply put it back in your drawer without washing it."

This time *his* jaw dropped open. But after a brief pause, a smirk crossed his face, and he chuckled. "No wonder I've had such a hard time getting my glasses clean!"

Unintentional errors. Mistakes. Some tickle our funny bone and make us laugh. Others haunt us and keep us awake in the middle of the night.

When I was lying in a hospital bed the morning after Nathan's birth, I heard the word "mistake." Only it wasn't funny at all. I'd never felt so confused in all my life.

I had just finished consulting with a physician. Still reeling from the news of my baby's condition, I looked at him and asked, "How did all of this happen?"

He did what he was supposed to do. Trying his best to comfort me, he gave me the medical and scientific explanation for Down syndrome and Nathan's heart problems. I'll never forget his closing comment.

"Mrs. Vredevelt, it was just a chromosomal anomaly, a genetic mishap, *a mistake...*"

I know this sincere man felt badly for us, and I know he wanted to alleviate any false guilt we might have had at the time. The "why's" of medical crises are sometimes as baffling to doctors as they are to patients. I was grateful for the compassion I saw in his eyes.

But when he left, I didn't know what to do with the information he'd given me.

A *mistake?*

Whose mistake?

I propped myself up with a few pillows and sat there in a stupor, overwhelmed by a mishmash of thoughts. How did his explanation fit with my faith? I didn't get it. How did Nathan's condition mesh with what I knew to be true from God's Word?

Psalm 139 says that God forms life in the womb. Did God make a mistake?

Defending myself against the pain, I intellectualized the ordeal. I reasoned with myself: "Okay Pam, this is how it works. You live in a fallen world, and your body isn't perfect. Your body made the mistake. Or perhaps the mistake occurred during the process of conception."

Logic didn't heal the pain. It rarely does.

Then my mind wandered ten years into the future. I saw Nathan coming home from school and asking, "Mom, how come I have Down syndrome?" I knew the standard medical explanation just wasn't going to cut it. I knew I could never say to him, "Nathan, the doctors tell us that the Down syndrome is just a mistake that happened when you were formed inside Mommy."

I decided right then and there that "mistake" was not a term our family would use to answer Nathan's hard questions. But at the same time I didn't know what I *would* say to him. My own disappointment with the diagnosis was so overwhelming I couldn't see myself saying to him, "Nathan, you have Down syndrome because it was part of God's plan for your life."

In the quietness of that hospital room I found myself secretly wondering if God might have made a mistake with Nathan after all. I was certain He had made a serious mistake giving *me* a child with special needs! I didn't feel capable of raising a mentally retarded son. I wasn't prepared for the task, and it wasn't the path I had chosen.

I know I'm not the only parent who struggles with fear and insecurity. Oh, the worn-out moms and dads I meet who in one way or another say, "God made a mistake when he gave us little Joe or little Susie." They don't feel capable. They're afraid they won't successfully raise their young. Feelings of inadequacy and failure overwhelm them as they struggle with the challenges of guiding a child with disabilities...hyperactivity...a strong will...a rebellious bent...or whatever heartache they bring with them into the counseling session.

I had to chuckle when one mother of three very unruly children was asked, "If you had it to do over again, would you have children?" Without skipping a beat she replied, "Oh, yes. Of course. Just not the same ones."

I recently talked with a pastor's wife who said to me, "God made a mistake when he assigned us to this ministry. Things went fine for a while, and then everything blew up in our face. God placed us on a team with a hostile individual who polarized our congregation. Now we're in the middle of a church split. We didn't have what the church needed to hold things together."

My response was, "Maybe your assignment wasn't to 'hold things together.' Maybe God wanted to do a new and different work in your town. Maybe God trusted you with this assignment because He knew you would remain faithful to His people when the conflicts occurred. Who's to say that the church split wouldn't have happened if someone else had been pastoring? Could it be that God gave you the job because He knew He could trust your perseverance and tenacity in the heat of the battle?"

How about you? Have you ever felt like God made a mistake in your life?

Maybe you didn't use those exact words but the idea was buried under thoughts beginning with the "if only's" we've already talked about:

- If only God had given me this talent or that ability...
- If only God had made me more like so-and-so...

- If only I didn't have this handicap or limitation…
- If only I weighed less…or was younger…or older…or had a better education…or better teeth…or a better figure…or a better childhood…or more money…
- If only such and such hadn't happened in my past, then I'd…

Why do such things happen? Does God make mistakes?

Shortly after we came home from the hospital with Nathan, Kay, a precious lady from our church, called. "I'm coming over to clean your house," she said. "What's a good day?"

She showed up on my doorstep a couple days later with our friend Idella. What a sight greeted my eyes when I opened the front door. These two looked like they'd just stepped off the set of a sci-fi movie with buckets on their heads, gas masks on their faces, combat boots, striped socks, and aprons to cover outfits that would have been rejected by the homeless.

They came to make me laugh. It worked!

But Kay and Idella's visit was far more significant to me than the laughter—or the clean floors and dusted furniture they left behind. Kay is the mother of two, Kurt and Kara. We'd known the family over many years because their son was in our youth group years ago when John and I worked with teenagers. Kara, their youngest, was born with cerebral palsy and over the years had gone through extensive surgeries. For twelve years Kay had walked the path I was just beginning.

When I saw her standing there in that crazy getup on my porch, smiling from ear to ear, I remembered the many times I'd seen her in the past and thought, *She has such burdens; how can she be so happy?*

I plopped myself in our big stuffed chair in the living room to nurse Nathan and said, "Kay, I'm struggling with something.

I don't know how to view Nathan's Down syndrome from God's perspective. How do you see it?"

Wise lady that she is, Kay didn't give me any simple platitudes or pat answers. Instead, she pointed me back to Scripture. One of the passages that had been meaningful to their family since Kara's birth, she told me, was John chapter 9. I had my copy of *The Message* at hand. Eager for answers, I immediately picked it up and began to read:

> Walking down the street, Jesus saw a man blind from birth. His disciples asked, "Rabbi, who sinned: this man or his parents, causing him to be born blind?"
>
> Jesus said, "You're asking the wrong question. You're looking for someone to blame. There is no such cause-effect here. Look instead for what God can do." (John 9:1–3, *The Message*)

God spoke to me through those verses on that brisk fall afternoon. He challenged me to shift my focus. He challenged me to quit trying to "figure it all out" and to believe that God wanted to accomplish specific purposes through the adjustments our family was making to welcome Nathan.

Look instead for what God can do.

I pondered those verses for a long time as I held Nathan that day. I wondered how the blind man felt before Jesus intercepted his life. My hunch is he assumed he would always be shrouded with darkness. Little did he know he was headed for historical significance. Little did he know that one day he would boldly stand before the religious leaders of the day, testifying of God's healing power in his life.

Who can give you and me the ability to believe we have a future?

God.

And who can give you and me the faith to believe our children are in God's hands...no matter what?

God.

Who can give us the faith to believe God will have His way in our children's lives when circumstances seem to be pointing another direction?

God.

God challenges you and me to have eyes of faith for ourselves, for our children, for our marriages, for our jobs, and for our ministries. He says: "For I know the plans I have for you.... They are plans for good and not for evil, to give you a future and a hope.... When you pray, I will listen. You will find me when you seek me, if you look for me in earnest" (Jeremiah 29:11–13, TLB).

God—with a full awareness of our weaknesses, wounds, handicaps, and disappointments—challenges us to place our trust in Him...*even when our hearts are breaking...even when our logic screams that He doesn't care or that He has made a terrible mistake.*

In the end He will use us in His own special way. He will orchestrate our unique divine assignments. And *nothing* can stop Him from achieving His purpose. In fact the very weaknesses we think "get in God's way" are often what He uses to display His glory!

Tony Campolo tells of a time in his life when God used a weak little boy with special needs to start a revival at a junior high camp. Tony wrote:

Everybody ought to be a counselor at junior high camp, just once. A junior high kid's concept of a good time is picking on people. And in this particular case, at this particular camp, there was a little boy who was suffering from cerebral palsy. His name was Billy. And they picked on him.

Oh they picked on him. As he walked across the camp with his uncoordinated body they would line up and imitate his grotesque movements. I watched him one day as he was asking for direction. "Which…way…is…the…craft…shop?" he stammered, his mouth contorting. And the boys mimicked in that same awful stammer. "It's over…there…Billy." And then they laughed at him. I was irate.

But my furor reached its highest pitch when on Thursday morning it was Billy's cabin's turn to give devotions. I wondered what would happen, because they had appointed Billy to be the speaker. I knew that they just wanted to get him up there to make fun of him. As he dragged his way to the front, you could hear the giggles rolling over the crowd. It took little Billy almost five minutes to say six words.

Jesus…loves…me…I…love…Jesus.

When he finished, there was dead silence. I looked over my shoulder and saw junior high boys bawling all over the place. A revival broke out in that camp after Billy's short testimony. And as I travel all over the world, I find missionaries and preachers who say, "Remember me? I was converted at that junior high camp."

We counselors had tried everything to get those kids interested in Jesus. We even imported baseball players whose batting averages had gone up since they had started praying. But God chose not to use the superstars. He chose a kid with cerebral palsy to break the spirits of the haughty. He's that kind of a God."[1]

God loves to use the simple things of this world to confound the wise. He loves to take ordinary people like you and me and accomplish the miraculous in spite of us. Jesus didn't pick the superstars for His assignments when He came to this earth. He took simple fishermen, crooked tax gatherers, prostitutes, persecutors of the church, touched their lives by the power of His Spirit, and accomplished the miraculous.

Ephesians 2:10 (NASB) says, "For we are His workmanship, created in Christ Jesus for good works, which God prepared beforehand, that we should walk in them."

You and I are God's workmanship. The Greek word translated *workmanship* here is *poiema*, which means a work of art or a specially designed product. As a matter of fact, it's the term from which we acquire our English word *poem*. Each one of us is God's special work of art. His poem. The verse goes on to say we are his work of art *for a reason*. We were created in Christ Jesus for good works, which He prepared ahead of time.

Guess what? God has some "good works" shoes that fit only you. They were custom-made in Heaven for your feet and yours alone. Don't try to give your shoes to Sam or Mary because you're afraid or you feel inadequate; you'll rob yourself of participating in some marvelous works of God. And don't try to wear Sam's or Mary's shoes, either. No matter how hard you try they won't fit, and you'll get blistering sores. God created shoes just for you and has predetermined assignments only you can carry out.

You are who you are by divine design. And with that divine design come divine assignments.

I'm convinced that a little boy with Down syndrome, by the name of Nathan Vredevelt, is a work of art. He has some special shoes that God designed just for him, to walk a path of divine purpose.

What are we going to say to Nathan when he is old enough to ask us about his Down syndrome? What will we say to him when someone else gives him the message that he's a misfit, a reject, a chromosomal anomaly, a genetic mishap, a mistake? What will we say to him when he hears that 99 percent of the babies like him are aborted before they ever get a chance to see the sunlight of this world? What will we say?

We will put him on our lap and wrap him in our arms and say something like this:

"Nathan, God made you very special. You have a special purpose in this world. You are not a mistake. You are who you are, by divine design. God created you in love. He called you into being at the right time and the right place. Did you know that before you were even formed in my womb God knew you? You were in God's heart and mind long before we found out you were going to be our baby. You are not an afterthought. You are a gift from God. You are a joy and a delight, not a disappointment.

"Nathan, you belong to our family. You are not an intrusion. When God looks at you, He smiles, because He created you in love.

"Sometimes people are hard on you because you don't do things as quickly as they do. But Nathan, everyone has strengths and weaknesses. And you have marvelous strengths where others are very, very weak. God has things for you to do in this world that others wouldn't have the patience to do.

"You are happy, always greeting us with a loving smile when you see us. Many people in this world aren't happy at all, Nathan. Did you know that?

"You are affectionate and generous with your hugs and kisses. Did you know that some people don't know how to share that kindness with others? That is one of your wonderful gifts.

"And Nathan, you are strong in spirit—where strength really counts. A spirit of praise and worship freely flows from your heart!

"Nathan, God has done miracles in your life. When you were born, you almost died. But you lived because God wanted you to live. He has important reasons for your being here. And when your heart wasn't functioning well, God's people prayed for you, and God healed your heart.

"Nathan, be proud of who you are, because God has His hand on your life.

"He loves you and we love you…and no one can ever take that away from you."

CHAPTER TWENTY-SEVEN

A GLIMPSE OF GLORY

Did I not tell you that if you believed,
you would see the glory of God?
JOHN 11:40

Years ago John and I had the privilege of traveling to the Far East with Nora Lam. We ministered in crusades and distributed Bibles to those hungry for God's Word behind the Bamboo Curtain.

It was the summer our first baby was due to arrive, had it lived to full term. The trip was a planned diversion during our grief.

According to the law of averages—or any other natural law you might choose—Nora Lam should be dead. Time and again she faced certain death, fleeing from Japanese-occupied Shanghai, only to suffer hunger and deprivation under the Communist regime. She endured forced labor, frequent beatings, and even faced a firing squad—only to be gloriously spared.

I remember being glued to my chair as I listened to her tell her astonishing story—

"One, two, three, FIRE!"

I heard the crack of rifles. I tensed for the impact of bullets ripping through my flesh. And I fell to the ground.

For a few seconds I lay motionless like the bodies in the field around me. Was this all there was to dying? The air was silent, except for the echo of shots still reverberating in the dusk.

Then a startling realization hit me. I was breathing. I wasn't dead. I was alive! But how could it be? What about the shots—the whine of bullets coming straight toward me? Communist sharpshooters never missed. What had happened?

The force of my fall had somehow loosened the ropes that tied my hands, and I wriggled them free and sat up, pulling the blindfold from my eyes. Yes, I could see…. I looked down at my clothes—no bullet holes, no blood. I felt my body—no new pain, no bullet-inflicted injury. I was alive.

The Communists jerked me to my feet, and shoved me back in the direction of the school. A short distance away, the firing squad stood as if it were frozen in place—or turned to stone—looking at me dumbfounded, as if they doubted I was real.

Next the interrogations began and the questions were angrier than ever:

"Why did the bullets come out from the guns and go over you and under you and around you, but not hit you?"

"What was the light that came down from the sky and blinded us so we couldn't see you?"

I knew the answer to that one.

"Jesus is the Light," I said.

"DON'T PREACH AT US!"

"I'm not preaching. I'm telling the truth, answering your question."[1]

In one of the darkest moments imaginable, Nora had a glimpse of God's glory. So did her captors—and to them, it was blinding!

Nora's story is one I hold dear to my heart. I have many memories about our trip to the Orient with her. Some put a smile on my face, like the little children begging for a Bible of their very own, and the times God healed the blind, deaf, dumb, and lame. But there was one day during the mission that was very difficult for me.

It was the day the baby we lost should have been born.

We went to a children's crusade in the morning; it was 100 degrees and 90 percent humidity—a bit too much for a West Coast girl! When we got back to the hotel after several hours in the steamy heat, I was dripping wet and exhausted. Several of the other team members made plans to go sightseeing, and John (bless his heart) was rarin' to go. I knew I didn't have another ounce of energy to spare, so I encouraged him to join the others while I went to the room to unwind.

I tried taking a nap but was too restless. So I pulled out my guitar and began to worship. Tears were streaming, but I was singing. All the grief of losing the baby came flooding back.

In the quietness of that little hotel room a song came to my heart...and I'll always believe it was from Him. I've never been a songwriter, but this simple little chorus would eventually be recorded and sung in churches all across the nation. But I knew nothing of that at the time. I only knew that I felt soothed and comforted—lifted for a time above my sadness.

O Lord my God I worship you.
You are my peace in this hour.
With outstretched arms I sing to You.

You are my strength and my power.
You reign on high; Almighty is Your name.
Glory! Glory! I give You Glory!
O Lord of Glory, I worship You.

That's the way it is. God gives us a glimpse of His glory
when we need it the most. Not when things are great. Not
when all is well. Not when our pathway is dappled with sunlight and lined with wildflowers. No, but rather…

when it's dark
when we're afflicted
when plans fall apart
when circumstances try to squeeze the life from us
when hell seems near
when we're obeying God's voice, even in our weakness
    and discouragement
when we're standing against the majority to fight for
    what is right
when we're choosing to believe, in spite of a deep long
    ing to throw in the towel
when life feels like one long string of mistakes
when we're enduring difficult people who make false
    accusations, chronic complaints, or don't see to care
when we're prying our fingers off of whatever we hold
    dear so that our hands are open to receive whatever
    God wants to give.

Paul faced many such situations. Perhaps that's why he
experienced glimpses of God's glory on so many occasions. It
gave him the courage to endure; it gave him strength to perse-
vere in *crushing* circumstances. He writes, "We do not lose

heart, but though our outer man is decaying, yet our inner man is being renewed day by day. For momentary, light affliction is producing for us an eternal weight of glory far beyond all comparison, while we look not at the things which are seen, but at the things which are not seen; for the things which are seen are temporal, but the things which are not seen are eternal" (2 Corinthians 4:16–18, NASB).

The year after Nathan was born was a very long year. His afflictions and those we shared as his parents seemed anything but "light" or "momentary." They seemed overwhelming—and interminable. Whenever I put my car in "drive," it automatically headed to the doctor's office. When I looked in the mirror, I could see the effects of stress. John and I felt ourselves aging years in a span of months. It was hard to sleep at night and even harder to get up in the morning. Jessie and Ben suffered, too. Any trauma affects the entire family.

Paul certainly had his fair share of trauma. There wasn't anything bad that didn't happen to that poor man. How did he do it? How did he belt out those songs in the dungeon at Philippi, with his back ripped to bloody ribbons by a Roman whip? What gave him the ability to refer to his troubles as "light" and "momentary"?

Perspective. Eternal perspective. My friend Ron Mehl, who has survived a major heart attack and suffered over a decade with active leukemia, writes:

How distressing and discouraging life becomes when we lose eternal perspective. It's as though we're trying to live on a flat piece of paper, in a two-dimensional world with no depth of meaning or anticipation or joy. We cannot "read" the Christian life on the basis of individual circumstances. We must not place our focus on individual events such as a heart attack, an illness, or an injury. If we do, we'll lose sight of the fact that there's a wider, deeper picture here. And it's an eternal one. It is a work that God is doing from beginning to end.[2]

As he endured unspeakable agonies, Paul rekindled his faith with visions of the glories to come. He set his sights forward. He focused on the unseen rather than the seen. That's what kept him going. And it's what can give you and me strength to face another day, too. Glory is on the way. First a few glimpses in our dark circumstances...and then...The Real Thing. Forever.

A well-known prophet tells us that the angels surrounding the Lord's heavenly throne call out to one another, saying: "Holy, Holy, Holy, is the LORD of hosts. *The whole earth is full of His glory"* (Isaiah 6:3, NASB).

Have you seen it? Have you caught a glimpse of His glory in the darkness of your circumstances? Some people journey through life and completely miss that point. Don't let that happen to you. Open your eyes. Watch for the times God uses little people to do BIG things. God wants to use you. So keep a lookout.

I don't know about you, but just one little glimpse of glory can keep this cracked pot beaming for a long time.

CHAPTER TWENTY-EIGHT

A Paradox, Bittersweet

...Sorrowful, yet always rejoicing;
poor, yet making many rich;
having nothing, and yet
possessing everything.

2 CORINTHIANS 6:10

A paradox, among other things, is a statement that seems contradictory.

In the past several years I have become aware of the "opposites" that coexist in my life. My experience has brought new meaning to the paradoxes I've read in Scripture during the last twenty-seven years I've known the Lord.

Life on this fallen planet is bittersweet. Joy and sorrow are inseparable. In the last five years my world has been opened to a whole new group of people I was not sensitive to before. Those with special needs have stolen my heart.

They have taught me about love and to take nothing for granted. I have never felt as much grief as I have felt in the last five years—and yet in all truth, I have never tasted such pleasure in the simple things of life.

I've despised those moments of feeling vulnerable and powerless; I much prefer feeling in control. But I am learning—oh, slowly, it seems—that control is really an illusion.

The bottom line? *I don't have to make my life work out.* Even the strange, the unplanned, and those things we call mistakes can harmoniously weave together for good in God's great plan.

Never have I felt so weak.

Never have I felt so strong.

Since Nathan arrived, I've held some private funerals to commemorate some of my own personal losses...

the death of my agenda for my life
the death of my dreams for a healthy baby
the death of a professional position
the death of creative writing for five years
the death of certain, once-cherished areas of ministry
the death of much of my free time
the death of a few relationships, due to lack of time and culti
    vation

Clearly I have had times when my own soul felt dead.

But in the same breath I can truly say I have never felt more alive. New life is springing up everywhere through the sodden ashes of the old. I sense new vitality when I'm with John and the kids, in the counseling office, and on assignment where God leads. New, hitherto-undiscovered gifts have emerged in ministry. I am more at home with myself and others. Acceptance and gratitude have found deep roots in my soul. I have fresh confidence that *I am where I am supposed to be* at this time in my life. And if God wants me in a different place, He'll orchestrate things to get me there.

Joy in sorrow. Strength in weakness. Light in darkness. Life in death. Angels behind rockers. Heavenly glory spilling out of cracked, earthenware jars.

It is His signature on our lives.

Now that you have finished *Angel behind the Rocker*...

Do you have a story about someone with special needs who has blessed your life? Can you tell me how? Has God ever intervened in your life in a way that defied human reason? (In other words, you knew beyond a doubt that it could only have been Him.) What happened? What did God teach you in the process? I'd love to hear from you! Please write me at:

Pam Vredevelt
P.O. Box 1093
Gresham, Oregon 97030

Chapter Thirteen
"Someone's Talking to Me"

1. Dr. Ron Mehl, *Surprise Endings* (Sisters, Ore.: Multnomah Publishers, Inc., 1993).

Chapter Eighteen
Accepting a New Destination

1. Emily Perl Kingley, from an October 1992 "Dear Abby" column.

Chapter Twenty-three
"The Gift of Letting Go"

1. Dr. Billy Graham, *Billy Graham: The Inspirational Writings* (Dallas, Tex.: Word, Inc., 1995).
2. Dr. Pamela Reeve, *Parables of the Forest* (Sisters, Ore.: Multnomah Publishers, Inc. 1989).

Chapter Twenty-five
A Path around the Swamp

1. Victor Frankl, *Man's Search for Meaning* (New York, N.Y., Touchstone Books, 1984).

Chapter Twenty-six
Did God Make a Mistake?

1. Tony Campolo, "Just a Kid with Cerebral Palsy," (*U Magazine*, April/May 1988).

CHAPTER TWENTY-SEVEN
A GLIMPSE OF GLORY

1. Nora Lam, *China Cry* (Nashville, Tenn.: Word, Inc., 1980), 21, 62, 63. Used by permission.
2. Dr. Ron Mehl, *Meeting God at a Dead End* (Sisters, Ore.: Multnomah Publishers, Inc., 1996).